> "Do not suppose that I have come to bring peace to the earth. I did not come to bring peace, but a sword. For I have come to turn a man against his father ... a daughter against her mother, a man's enemies will be the members of his own household." (Matthew 10:34-36)

THE LIE AND
THE LIGHT
America/Divided

James L. Ellsberry

MASTERSWORDS BOOKS

2018

THE LIE AND
THE LIGHT
America/Divided

By James Ellsberry: 1st Edition

All rights reserved under Title 17, U.S. Code, International and Pan-American Copyright Conventions. No part of this work may be reproduced or transmitted in any form or by any means, electronic or mechanical, including but not limited to photocopying, scanning, recording, broadcast or live performance, or duplication by any information storage or retrieval system without prior written permission from the publisher, except for the inclusion of brief quotations with attribution in a review or report. To request permission contact the author's site.

This book is publicly offered contingent on the reader's prior agreement that the author(s) and publisher(s) accept no responsibility of any kind for conclusions reached by readers of this book. The opinions expressed by the author should not necessarily be regarded as representative of any past employer, friends, relatives, advisors, or organization with whom he has been affiliated. If you do not agree with these terms, you may return this book unread for a full refund. Contact jells3344@gmailcom.

Ω

Copyright © 2018, by James Ellsberry, 1st Edition

Acknowledgments

My gratitude to Pastor Bruce Bendinger, and elders, Rick Ransdell and Dave Julius, at *New Beginnings Community Church,* Franklin, IN, for their support and encouragement as I struggled to get this book completed.

A special thank you to Dan Snow, Brown County Career Center, for sharing his knowledge and experience as an author and publisher. Thanks to my wife, Doris, and our children, Stephen, Lee Anne, and Karen Michelle; they always offer strength and confidence when I'm about ready to throw in the towel.

And to Howard and Dorothy, and my sister Marianne; they loved me when I wasn't worthy.

All praise and glory to God, who answered my prayers when I was lost, provided words when they wouldn't come to me, and has given me the courage to speak out in His Truth.

Nothing is accomplished in a vacuum; this book would never have been published without those mentioned above reminding me that the gift I have was given to be shared with others.

"Neither do men light a candle and hide it under a bushel, but, place it on a candlestick that it gives light to all who are in the house." (Matthew 5:15)

JLE

Contents

Acknowledgments 4

Preface 7

Part One   Conflicting Worldviews: 12

What is Truth: *Why it Matters* 13

In the Beginning: *Sin Enters the World* 22

The Nature of Sin: *Twisting the Truth* 24

Who Is God? *Truth Revealed* 29

Who is Jesus? *God in Human Flesh* 49

America the Beautiful: *Taken Captive by the Lie* 62

Part Two   Six Lies: *That Changed America* 63

1859 - Charles Darwin: *Children of God or Goo* 64

The Spread of Darwinism: *Social Consequences* 68

The Spread of Darwinism: *Unintended Consequences* 71

The Spread of Darwinism: *Public Education and* ....
Socialism 75

1953 - Hugh Hefner: *The Playboy Culture* 80

1963 - Madalyn Murray O'Hair: *God Expelled from School* 88

1971: The Pentagon Papers: *Lies Revealed* 101

1973: Roe v. Wade: *Abortion on Demand* 110

2015: Sphere Sovereignty: *Trashing Individual*............
Rights..119

Part Three   Religion on Trial............................166

Religion or Humanism? *Shall Christians Testify?*....167

About the Author: ***Other Books by Jim***.................193

THE LIE AND

THE LIGHT

America/Divided

MASTERSWORDS BOOKS 2018

Preface

America is succumbing to a lie. It's a subtle lie, as old as humanity itself. It is the innate trust we have in ourselves. The belief that our human powers, intelligence, imagination, creativity, courage, and physical skills are sufficient to overcome any challenge that confronts us, just bring it on! Clearly, we are the dominant species, masters over all creatures on earth.

This belief has plagued humankind from its earliest beginnings, and we keep repeating the same mistake again and again. Great civilizations rise, but eventually, the lie takes captive the hearts and minds of the people. Although remnants will remain, most of what was achieved will have been poisoned.

The Roman Empire (27 BC-1453 AD), Ancient Egypt (3150 BC-30 BC), Ottoman Empire (1299-1908 AD), and Chinese Empire (221 BC-1912 AD), all prevailed thousands of years longer than has the United States. Their stories are well documented; no need for details. The point is that history reveals we humans have been incapable of coming together, as a nation, under any form of government, and successfully sustaining our collective identity indefinitely.

Never, before 1776, had a people voluntarily assembled themselves to form a government based on the concept of self-rule, emphasizing the unalienable rights of individual citizens. The "great American experiment," it has been called, and that fact alone has made America vulnerable to suffer from internal strife. The record makes clear, the prideful egos of all but a handful of sultans, kings, and monarchs have been no better than the openly brutish dictators and despots, that through the centuries, even to the present, have shown no qualms about starving, imprisoning, torturing, and murdering citizens daring to question even a word of their authority.

So, the question becomes, when faced with a sorely divided people, corruption and failure in high places, will a democratic republic, constituted on principles of equality for all, under the law, a government of the people and by the people, confront the lie that can destroy it?

Dynasties, empires, and kingdoms, that have gone before us, have largely swallowed the lie and ignored the Truth. The question before us today should be of grave concern to everyone that claims to love America.

"...Every kingdom divided against itself is brought to desolation, and every city or house divided against itself will not stand." (Matthew 12: 22-28)

Introduction

When asked about the direction in which America appears to be headed, roughly two-thirds of us believe we're headed in the wrong direction. This is old news; opinion polls have reported this disconnect for more than a decade. Getting two-thirds of Americans to agree on anything is rather astonishing. The problem with getting agreement on this question is that it doesn't reveal anything about which direction we should be headed. Left, right, up, down, east, west, is there any agreement on what people believe is the proper path? Is it possible to restore a sense of unity and civility that would enable our government to function as our Forefathers intended? Gridlock in Washington has become a problem!

Politics has long been recognized as a rough game, played primarily by those with big egos, thick skin, and mostly good intentions. Those brave souls entering the game, lacking those prerequisite qualities, toughen up quickly, or they're one and done. In the early years of our nation's history, those bold enough to serve never dreamed of making a lifetime career of politics. Now it's commonplace for individuals to "serve" in Washington, D.C., the entirety of their adult lives. This phenomenon has become a problem!

Compounding that matter is the increasing number of Americans dependent on the elect of Capitol Hill to solve their problems. Too many have been taught to believe they're entitled to government handouts, rather than pull themselves up by their boot straps. The attitude of relying on government to provide for us from the cradle to the grave has become a problem!

America, from its beginning, has been a nation founded on the principle that everyone has an equal right to protection under the law. Our Forefathers recognized the fallen nature of humans. We are flawed; we can't be trusted to always do what is right. They acknowledged that evil exists in the hearts of mankind; therefore, our *Constitution*, was amended to include a *Bill of Rights* protecting citizens from evil overreach by government.

Unfortunately, we are seeing that those who are the elect, are unwilling to bring charges against colleagues, who appear to have clearly violated federal law(s), thereby, establishing a double standard under the laws of the land. This inequity has become a problem!

Our Forefathers debated, argued, even resorted to fist fights, over issues they understood were crucial to laying the foundation for a government of the people, for the people, and by the people. Never, in mankind's history, had self-government been attempted.

These men were Christians. The *Holy Bible*, God's word, was the standard by which all things were measured. Did that make them perfect? Of course not. Were they corruptible, hypocritical? No more, or less than we. The point is, they agreed on the direction for the country. The standard they used was incorruptible. We have strayed from that standard; that has become a problem!

The intent of the message that is the foundation of this book, is simply to put forth evidence of game changing moments in our nation's history, that have led many to reject the truth claims of God, in favor of the false promises and lies of this world. Whether anyone likes it, or not, the principles upon which our nation was conceived were authored by men – men who believed in the word of God, recorded in the *Holy Bible* as the source of all Truth. The elegance of their words expresses their faith and trust in their Creator.

"We hold these truths to be self-evident, that all men are created equal, that they are endowed by their Creator with certain unalienable Rights, that among these are Life, Liberty and the pursuit of Happiness. ——"

Second Continental Congress, July 4, 1776

To get to the root cause of the bitterness, violence, and unforgiving tone that grips America, we must acknowledge that our growing disbelief, seeing God as irrelevant, gives license to sinful behavior and hateful attitudes. If there are no sacred, moral, or ethical standards, no consequences enforced for violating the law, then chaos reigns. If every person's beliefs are equally valid, the law of the jungle will prevail.

Sin is not a popular word in America, let alone any serious discussion about its consequences. That has become a problem!

Part One

Conflicting Worldviews: *What is Truth?*

"There is no God, and there is no soul. Hence, there are no needs for the props of traditional religion."

John Dewey (1859 –1952)
Humanist, "Father of American Education"

www.pinterest.com

"To this end was I born, and for this cause came I into the world, that I should bear witness unto the truth. Every one that is of the truth heareth My voice."
(John: 18:37)

Jesus of Nazareth, Son of God

https://www.youtube.com/watch?v=mzBxoaR6fnA

What is Truth?

Why it Matters

Veritology is a word you won't find in the dictionary. It's a word introduced by Del Tackett, host of the DVD series *The Truth Project*, produced by Focus on the Family (2006). Dr. Tackett was looking for a word to define the study of truth. A little research led him to explain how he was able to coin the word. "I decided I would do some combining ... I took the Latin term for truth, *veritas* and combined it with the derivation of the Greek suffix, *logos* and the merger resulted in *Veritology*, the *study of truth.*"

> "Morality is the basis of things and truth is the substance of all morality."
>
> Mahatma Gandhi

Why does truth matter? The answer seems obvious. In the absence of truth there is only confusion and chaos. Without Truth (with a capital T), everyone's version of what is true is as good as the next. Certainly, groups of like-minded people could agree on a version of truth that satisfies them, but then how many other groups would disagree, believing it's their version of the truth that should be accepted? You see the problem.

There are individuals and groups who worship at the altar of tolerance in the flawed belief that all views should be respected equally. I can't agree. When talking about what is true, let's not mistakenly believe that tolerance means all versions of truth are equally valid. We're living in a time when it's fashionable for individuals and groups to declare themselves and their agendas to be all kinds of things. You can declare yourself a rabbit and organize a pride day parade. Your right to do so is respected and guaranteed by the *First Amendment, Constitution of the United States.* It doesn't guarantee Truth.

In America, we have reached a point where it has become nearly impossible to separate truth from fiction or separate fiction from outright lies. Never, in human history, have people had immediate access 24/7/365 to "breaking news." Satellites, the internet, social media, personal computers, and iPHONEs, have combined to provide words and images from almost any location on earth. The speed of modern communication technology is measured in nanoseconds (one billionth of a second). It has revolutionized communication on all levels.

Like most things, whatever has the potential to be a strength, when overdone, becomes a liability. This is true of present-day communication. It's fast, timely, and accurate. All are essential elements of communication. The element that has become the stumbling block is accuracy. Technology is extremely accurate in its capacity to send, receive, and retrieve information. But, so far, in its development, it can only process what the human operator provides in the way of input—garbage in, garbage out. Voila! Fake news! Lies, scammers, hackers—trouble.

As a communications tool, social media has demonstrated unprecedented appeal around the globe. People everywhere are interacting with devices that put almost any information, about almost anything, right at their fingertips. It should be revolutionizing how, when, and where our children are educated. A fantastic tool, unlimited opportunity, but there is a dark side to the miracles of modern technology.

Facebook, Twitter, email, YouTube, so many options available for anyone desiring to post personal news items, including photos, videos, or share an article of interest with friends or relatives. Harmless fun, convenient, staying connected is a good thing. Not so fast, the evils supported by the internet include cyber bullying, pornography, stolen identity, and misinformation. We see and understand the truth about the ugly side of humanity.

> "A lie gets halfway around the world before the truth has a chance to get its pants on."
>
> Winston Churchill

There's another internet phenomenon, subtler in its impact on society than the three cited above. It's become known as "urban legends." Stories are circulated on the internet posing as fact. Usually, the information carries a grain of truth, but the goal is to sensationalize, exaggerate, distort the truth and inflame the issue. Some are humorous, but frequently they target the credibility of leaders of political parties, government policies, the police, or racial, ethnic, and religious issues. Such stories seldom identify a specific source or a byline; never the less, intelligent people are duped by urban legends, especially when the target is someone or something they don't like in the first place.

When the impact of urban legends is coupled with the unbridled power of biased internet platforms that can censor posts they don't like, silencing voices that disagree with their bias, internet providers join syndicated news agencies that have abandoned standards of journalism, the truthfulness of the news becomes questionable. Objective reporting has too often been replaced by opinion, unvetted reports, or false narratives from "anonymous" sources. Sound bites are preferable to substance, pinning derogatory labels on individuals and groups is acceptable, sleaze sells, and lies travel farther and faster than truth.

Seth Borenstein, Associated Press, reported the findings of researchers at the *Massachusetts Institute of Technology*. In the largest study of online misinformation, and funded by Twitter, the research team studied 126,000 stories that were tweeted millions of times between 2006 and 2016. They reported that fake news in all categories of information, sped through Twitter farther, faster, deeper, and more broadly than truth. False claims override the truth and freedom of speech in America is being threatened.

This is the minefield readers face in search of the truth. Who can we believe? Sadly, over the past half-century far too many of our nation's leaders have been guilty of lying to us, making us even more skeptical of the daily news. We should not be surprised. A warning has been given that these times would come.

"For the time will come when people will not put up with sound doctrine. Instead, to suit their own desires, they will gather around them a great number of teachers to say what their itching ears want to hear. They will turn their ears away from the truth and turn aside to myths. But you, keep your head in all situations, endure hardship, do the work of an evangelist, discharge all the duties of your ministry." (2 Timothy 4:3-5)

This is at the heart of the issue that has split America. The time has come. The people of one worldview believe strongly that God exists, place their faith in His word, and trust in His Absolute Truth. God rules over all. His laws are universal and immutable.

In opposition to this belief are increasing numbers of people, unbelievers, whose worldview rejects the reality of a living God, creator of all things. They believe in the intelligence, logic, imagination, courage, and basic goodness of mankind to rule with wisdom. As John Dewey, a respected humanist, stated, "There is no God, and there is no soul. Hence, there are no needs for the props of traditional religion."

British atheist, Richard Dawkins explains, "Evolution is a fact, as securely established as any in science, and he who denies it betrays woeful ignorance and lack of education, which likely extends to other fields as well. Evolution is not some recondite backwater of science, ignorance of which would be pardonable. It is the stunningly simple but elegant explanation of our very existence and the existence of every living creature on the planet." (http://azquotes.com/quotes/575073)

These opposing views seem irreconcilable. As the warning predicted, each group is surrounding itself with "teachers" who support what their own "itching ears" want to hear. Each holding to its own beliefs, turning away, rejecting the other. Only one can be the Truth. Either God is who He says He is, or not. Either Charles Darwin's theory of evolution is true, or not. Regardless of Dawkin's claim, evolution is not a scientific fact—it is a theory. Great faith is required on the part of those on either side of the divide. Which is Truth? Which is fable?

At this point, I want to be clear. I have no animus toward atheists, agnostics, or humanists, or any individual worldview that differs from mine. Earlier in my life, I subscribed to the fundamental tenets of humanism. However, my journey has led back to The Cross, and I'm writing from the perspective of a Christian's worldview.

I respect anyone's right to disagree with any claims I'm making; It is not my intent to insult, demean, or offend those who walk a different path. I trust readers to respect my attempt to bring to light six issues that have divided us, to clarify their consequences to America's social order, and to have readers thoughtfully consider what they believe, why they believe, and how those beliefs enrich the quality of their lives and the lives of others.

It's time for America to awaken from its spiritual coma, come to its senses, and acknowledge that there is only one source of Truth. All are free to deny that fact, oppose it with all their strength, but it will not change the authenticity of that reality.

God understands our flawed condition. He came into the world in human form, Jesus of Nazareth, the Messiah (Christ), who took the sins of all upon himself. He was rejected, mocked, persecuted and crucified, giving every drop of blood as atonement for our sin. Again, all can decide for themselves if this story is true.

Before discarding the idea that the Gospel message has no place in the modern world, consider this. The *Holy Bible* records the fact that Jesus stood before Pontius Pilate, the Roman governor of Judaea, accused of treason and being a political threat to Rome. In questioning Jesus about his activities, Pilate exclaimed, *"You are a king, then!"* *Jesus answered, "You say that I am a king. In fact, the reason I was born and came into the world is to testify to the truth. Everyone on the side of truth listens to me."* (John 18:37)

This, perhaps, is the most important verse in the Bible. Jesus said the reason he came into the world was to *"testify to the truth."* If that statement, made to a Roman governor, given the authority to execute criminals, is not true, then Jesus is a liar and Christianity is a farce. If you are not a believer, that statement should give you pause to think. He also said, *"I am the way, and the truth, and the life; no one comes to the Father, but through me."* (John 14:6)

These are outrageous claims made by Jesus. Why didn't Pilate and the Pharisees (Jewish spiritual leaders, enemies of Jesus) simply ignore him, and write him off as a nut case? Could it have been because they knew he was who he claimed to be?

We should be persuaded that a man does not give up his life for a lie. Of the eleven apostles sent out to testify to the Truth they had witnessed firsthand, ten endured horrific deaths at the hands of authorities. Only John was believed to have succumbed to old age. We are compelled to ask, why would any reasonable person submit to torture and death, when all one would have to do is deny the Truth?

> ...Jesus said, "If you hold to my teaching, you are really my disciples. Then you will know the truth, and the truth will set you free."
>
> John 8: 31-32

We can safely conclude that God is the source of all Truth. As Gandhi was quoted, "Truth is the substance of all morality," therefore, without Truth there can be no morality, and in the absence of morality, there can be no justice. The powerful will prevail over the weak, and there will be one set of laws for those who rule, and another set for those who are ruled.

Wake up America. Our government is tilting in favor of man's law. The Law beyond the law, upon which our Forefathers built this nation, is being superseded by those who believe their wisdom is greater than the Creator's.

There is nowhere to get relief from a government that has become so gargantuan in scope that it has become unmanageable. The three branches appear completely ineffective in their capacity to monitor and rein in each other when one exceeds its authority, encroaching on the sovereignty of the others. In recent years, we've seen presidents of both parties legislating by executive order—not what our Forefathers intended.

Congress, paralyzed by party politics, has devolved into a dysfunctional body devoid of leadership, unable to agree on which of the nation's laws ought to be enforced. Both houses have failed to set aside partisan politics in favor of doing what is best for America; the Supreme Court has filled that void by legislating from the bench. In a stunningly egregious decision, for the sake of political correctness, the Court granted itself the authority to redefine the sanctity of holy matrimony. In the meantime, states' rights are being preempted by Washington liberals with a socialist agenda. This is what happens when God's laws are cast aside in favor of man's law. Truth suffers—look for chaos and confusion to get even worse.

Do not plot evil against each other, and do not love to swear falsely. I hate all this," declares the LORD. (Zechariah 8:17)

In America, the decreasing role that religion plays in contemporary life leads me to believe there are many who are aware of God but have little understanding of His nature. Likely, most have at least heard of Jesus, but even among church-goers, more than a few have little understanding of the significance of the life of Jesus. Both are inextricably bound together in a relationship that addresses mankind's sinful nature. We can't speak about a divided America without establishing the reality of sin.

> *There is no surer sign of decay in a country than to see the rites of religion held in contempt.*
>
> Niccolo Machiavelli
> 1469-1527

"Surely the arm of the LORD is not too short to save, nor his ear too dull to hear. But your iniquities have separated you from your God; your sins have hidden his face from you, so that he will not hear. For your hands are stained with blood, your fingers with guilt. Your lips have spoken falsely, and your tongue mutters wicked things. No one calls for justice; no one pleads a case with integrity. They rely on empty arguments, they utter lies; they conceive trouble and give birth to evil." (Isaiah 59:1-4)

These prophetic words of Isaiah were spoken to people approximately 700 years before Christ came into the world. It seems to me as if he's speaking to America today.

In the Beginning:
Sin Enters the World

And he said to the woman, "Has God indeed said, you shall not eat of every tree of the garden? Then the serpent said to the woman, "You will not surely die. For God knows that in the day you eat of it your eyes will be opened, and you will be like God, knowing good and evil." (Genesis 3: 1-6)

Whether one is a person of faith or not, surely, we can agree there is evil in the world. It is the counterpoint to goodness. The flip sides of a coin; they do battle. Some have referred to it as a "cosmic battle," that has raged since the dawn of humanity. The lore of ancient cultures describes epic battles, taking place when time began, or even before, forces of good against forces of evil, fighting for control of our planet. Popular contemporary films and literature often pit these forces against one another, for control of the universe itself, at some time in the future.

Acknowledging the reality of evil is less a problem than agreeing to the origin of evil, and man's propensity for engaging in evil. Christians believe the verse above explains how evil entered the world. Eve was tempted by a liar who led her, and Adam, into an egregious sin against God.

Perhaps, if we wanted to cut them some slack, as we are wont to do when we mess up, we might say, they were naïve; God should have given them a second chance.

But, no, God's nature is pure; His standard for obedience is without question.

When Adam and Eve traded God's word for the lie, that they could be like gods, that transaction changed the relationship between man and God forever. Mankind, thus, degenerated into a fallen state, and that's where we remain today. *"for all have sinned and fall short of the glory of God…"* (Romans 3:23)

This point, the nature of mankind, is one that divides America. There are those, that take offense at the idea that mankind's basic nature is flawed from the beginning. Others don't have a clue, and don't care, and some, at the very core of their being, care deeply and live to re-establish a relationship with the One they regard as their Creator.

Who is man? Who is God? What is sin? What is truth? These questions are not rhetorical; how one answers reflects one's worldview. Not having an answer, likewise, is a reflection, of how one sees the world, and his or her place in it. These fundamental questions are not for one's intellect alone, but of the spirit, and of raw emotion.

Throughout history, and to this day, bitter wars, injustice, and terrible crimes against humanity have erupted over these questions. There are some who don't want to hear anything about God, or sin, or a worldview. We remain divided, and that division is one of the main reasons America, as we have known it, is at risk.

The Nature of Sin:
Twisting the Truth

On July 30, 1956, President Dwight D. Eisenhower, signed P. L. 84-851, passed by the 84th Congress of the United States, and declaring the words, *"In God We trust,"* were to be written on our currency and become our national motto. That act acknowledged our heritage as a Godly nation. So, why is it so hard to trust in God—easier said than done.

Some unbelievers, and some Christians, find it difficult to accept the concept of original sin. Sin is not a word that gets used much anymore. We don't like to think of humankind as having a flawed character right from the get-go. It's hard to think of an "innocent" baby lying in a cradle as a "sinner." Yet, it is so.

"Therefore, just as through one man, sin entered the world, and death through sin, and thus death spread to all men, because all sinned." (Romans 5:12)

Sin had its beginning in the Garden. It's not just an ancient fable; the nature of sin is relevant today. It's a story as old as humankind and keeps getting replayed over, and over again. Temptation existed then, and it exists today, as strong as ever. In the flesh, we are weak. We cave in to our sinful nature so easily, and in so many subtle ways. We don't have to be "bad" to be a sinner. We can be led into sinful behavior by trusting in the wrong words from the wrong people. That's exactly what happened to Adam and to Eve.

The serpent (evil) spoke to Eve as a "friend," pointing out to her how selfish God had been to provide all the fruits of the garden only to deny them one.

He convinced her that she and Adam should be entitled to enjoy it all, the *Tree of Knowledge* included. Rather than believe, trusting in the Word of God, Eve chose to trust in the word, accept the advice, of a liar. Then, Adam erred in the same way, choosing to trust Eve's word, that eating of the fruit would not harm them.

It sounded good, tasted good, probably felt good. But, therein lies our problem. God clearly told them to abstain; they didn't trust Him, and their rebellion changed our human nature forever. We can trust God; God is good, loves us, but it is our nature to "spin" His words, ever so slightly, twisting their meaning to align with our own desires.

But, those innocent babies haven't sinned, many will say. They're blameless and have committed no evil. That's where we've missed the point. Sin is like a genetic disease, and we're all born with a terminal case of it. However, the symptoms may not be revealed in the same way, or in the same time for each of us.

For example, let's say we're victims of a disease—cancer. As with sin, it seems there are many kinds and degrees of cancer. One may have cancer of the lungs and die within a few months. Another might have breast cancer, get treatment and be in remission. One might have skin cancer, get treatment, and live a long healthy life, bearing, perhaps, a few scars. Another might have bone cancer, lose a jawbone resulting from surgery, and be permanently disfigured. The same disease attacking all, but varying forms and degrees of suffering and recovery.

As individuals, we make comparisons about the symptoms we see. Well, we might say, my cancer's not as bad as hers, or, I look better than he does. In the same way, we rationalize the severity of our sinful condition. My sins aren't as atrocious as those of Pol Pot, Adolph Hitler, or Joseph Stalin. I haven't committed any heinous murders such as those by Jeffrey Daumer or Richard Speck. Never the less, I'm still diseased. It's just that the symptoms of my sinful nature are less obvious. I cling to that fact, in the hope that God will cut me the same slack that I cut for myself.

The problem is, I know I'm guilty of two things: first, unlike cancer, I have a choice as to whether I want it. Second, I'm guilty of lying to myself about the ugliness I bear, and I know it. In God's eye's, sin is sin. He doesn't make distinctions or quantify it. Thank God for His amazing grace. I trust in His word, that although unearned and undeserved, I am saved by His grace alone, not sparing the life of His son to take away my sins. That Truth shapes my view of the world and how things work.

In America, over the past fifty years, the nation's opinion polls have revealed a significant downward trend in religion. Fewer people are identifying with formal church affiliation and attending services. A second trend, that should be disturbing to all who profess to love our country, is the increasing belief that church and religion have little relevance to contemporary life. Why, then, bother to have any concern for trusting in God, when God is perceived as irrelevant to one's quality of life?
(https://news.gallup.com/poll/1690/religion.aspx)

"But how are they to call on him in whom they have not believed? And how are they to believe in him of whom

they have never heard? And how are they to hear without someone preaching to them?" (Romans 10:14)

The Ten Commandments are understood by most of us to be laws, not rules, not suggestions, but laws, broken under the penalty of death. Again, it's easy to miss the point. We are already condemned. The wages of sin is death. But, another way to look at the *Commandments* is to think of them as a prescription for healing our disease.

Just as a trained physician might prescribe surgery, chemotherapy, radiation, or some other method, to defeat the ravages of cancer, God has provided His Holy Spirit as a means for treating the sinful nature we have from birth.

We can trust God. He has promised that whosoever believes in Him shall have everlasting life. We can't do it on our own. Only in God's love can we find salvation.

"Because greater is He who is us than he who is in the world." (1 John 4:4)

On our own, we remain in our nakedness, reluctant, perhaps, ashamed to be seen by others as we truly know ourselves. Misguided by vanity and denial, some try to become great on their own.

"And those who exalt themselves shall be humbled; those who humbles themselves shall be exalted." (In the kingdom of God.) (Matthew 23:12)

We need the medicine of the Church to help us treat our disease. In seeking God's presence, we are empowered by His love, inspired by the support of others (also born again of the Spirit), and by His grace our sins forgiven. America, take note. Our sins are real; we are slowly exchanging God's Truth, for the empty promises, and lies of this world.

"But now the righteousness of God apart from the law is revealed, ... through faith in Jesus Christ, to all and on all who believe. For there is no difference; for all have sinned and fall short of the glory of God" (Romans 3:21-23)

The unbelievers likely find that verse offensive or childish because one of their core beliefs is that you don't have to have God to be good. Mature, competent educated adults are quite capable of leading fulfilling, self-directed lives without God as their psychological crutch.

I confess, there was a time I subscribed to that idea, but when I lost my roadmap and came to a fork in the road, I put my faith in the one less traveled. Truth is—as Frost has written, "It has made all the difference."

Self-centered indulgence, pride and a lack of shame over sin are now emblems of the American lifestyle.

Billy Graham 1918 – 2018

American Evangelist

Who Is God?
Truth Revealed

God said to Moses, "I AM WHO I AM. This is what you are to say to the Israelites: I AM has sent me to you. The LORD, *the God of your fathers—the God of Abraham, the God of Isaac and the God of Jacob—has sent me to you … This is my name forever … the name you shall call me— from generation to generation."* (Exodus 3: 13-15)

These are the words spoken by God when He called Moses to go before the elders of Israel and tell them that I AM, had spoken, and they would go before Pharaoh telling him to release the Israelites from their bondage in Egypt.

For many reasons, there are people who reject the reality of God. Chief among these is that since no one has seen God, and man has yet to prove absolutely that He exists, their intellect will not allow them to consider anything as real, beyond their senses or knowledge of the physical world. Therefore, a virgin giving birth to a child born of a spirit father, and becoming a child prodigy, teaching and prophesying in the Jewish Temple, performing miraculous acts that defy science, including restoring the dead to life, and upon becoming an adult, is executed, buried, and three days later, returns to give instructions to his disciples before ascending into the heavens. All of that requires too much for unbelievers; their sense of what is reasonable doesn't stretch that far. It's understandable; a lot of us have been there.

Others of those who choose to reject God have read or heard the Gospel message and found it disturbing. How, they ask, could a God that is said to be loving and compassionate allow innocent children to be abused, slaughtered, or born with terrible defects? They question, how a caring God would continue to allow evil to exist in the form of horrific wars, killing billions worldwide? Have not wars been conducted in His name, they ask? Why do bad things happen to good people, even to those who profess to believe? What kind of father asks his son to die for him, they ask? Christians have answers to these questions.

These questions, and others like them, are relevant to understanding the nature of God's character. For humans to speculate on God's divine qualities presents a lot of challenges, not the of least of which are the limits imposed by language and vocabulary. Therefore, let's begin with the question: Is God who He says He is? We can keep opinions and speculation to a minimum by studying what God has revealed to us about Himself through His word.

"In the beginning God created the heavens and the earth. Now the earth was formless and empty, darkness was over the surface of the deep, and the Spirit of God was hovering over the waters." (Genesis 1:1)

Unbelievers will likely scoff, but they shouldn't be concerned; after all, if there is no God, as they believe, then anything that follows is irrelevant. To explain the origin of life, and all things created, unbelievers most likely worship at the altar of evolution. Modern science has dispelled the science of Charles Darwin's landmark book, *On the Origin of Species.* It was published in 1859, long before today's hi-tech science that has been able to reveal the astonishing complexity contained in a single living cell. New knowledge has reduced Darwinian evolution to a horse and buggy explanation of the origin of life. Clearly, it requires as much faith, even more so perhaps, to accept Darwin' theory as it does creationism.

God is eternal. It is God's nature that He existed before time began. Genesis 1 is supported by another verse. *"'I am the Alpha and the Omega,' says the Lord God, 'who is and who was and who is to come, the Almighty.'"* (Revelation 1:8) We can state with certainty that God is eternal, the beginning and the end. It may seem a contradiction to say God is eternal (never-ending), and then say, God is the Omega (the end of all things). The end can mean the end of all things that exist in time; eternity is not bound by time. Throughout eternity, God remains the same, unchanging. *"Jesus Christ is the same yesterday and today and forever."* (Hebrews 13:8). *"Every good gift and every perfect gift is from above, coming down from the Father of lights with whom there is no variation or shadow due to change."* (James 1:17)

God is multi-dimensional. God's persona is often referred to as *The Trinity*, that he exists in three dimensions, God the Father, God the Son (Jesus as he appeared in human form), God the Holy Spirit. It's beyond our capacity to truly grasp this quality. Unbelievers, therefore, dismiss it as something only the ignorant or superstitious would subscribe to. How can anything exist as three separate and distinct things, and yet, be an integrated whole?

A logical question. Many minds greater than mine have attempted to explain this phenomenon in a way that relates to our human experience. Chemically, water exists, as a unified whole, H_2O, but it can also exist as ice, a solid, and steam, as an invisible gas. You can criticize this as overly simplistic, but it does suggest the possibility of a superhuman having a nature of far greater complexity than our own. *"Jesus looked at them and said, "With man this is impossible, but with God all things are possible.'"* (Matthew 19:26) We should be careful not to dismiss what we don't understand.

God is the Creator. Genesis 1:1 states that God created the heavens and the earth, but there's much more to add. *"The heavens declare the glory of God; And the firmament shows His handiwork. Their line has gone out through all the earth, And their words to the end of the world. In them He has set a tabernacle for the sun."* (Psalm 19:1-4)

God created the earth and entrusted us to rule over His creations, and to be responsible for their care. Originally, God's gift to us was Eden, a garden paradise, but we got caught up in the lies of evil. We disobeyed our covenant with God. When Adam and Eve were banished from the garden, fallen from grace, the earth was cursed, and our stewardship became more difficult.

"For by Him all things were created that are in heaven and that are on earth, visible and invisible, whether thrones or dominions or principalities or powers. All things were created through Him and for Him." (Colossians (1:16)

"By faith we understand that the universe was created by the word of God, so that what is seen was not made out of things that are visible." (Hebrews 11:3)

God spoke the universe into being. Before you laugh at this remarkable feat, or declare it impossible, or question His authority, you might check out Job, chapters 38-42. God has some questions for all of us to ponder. He has made His awesome power clear for all to see. We are without excuse.

God is sovereign. God is in complete control of all that He has created. He has absolute power and authority over every aspect of all that has been, is, or ever will be, as in—eternal.

"For my thoughts are not your thoughts, neither are your ways my ways," declares the LORD. "As the heavens are higher than the earth, so are my ways higher than your ways and my thoughts than your thoughts.

As the rain and the snow come down from heaven, and do not return to it without watering the earth and making it bud and flourish, so that it yields seed for the sower and bread for the eater, so is my word that goes out from my mouth. It will not return to me empty but will accomplish what I desire and achieve the purpose for which I sent it." (Isaiah 55:8-11)

God is omniscient. God is all-knowing. Christians believe God knows all things past, present, and future. His knowledge and wisdom are unlimited. *"Oh, the depth of the riches and wisdom and knowledge of God! How unsearchable are his judgments and how inscrutable His ways!"* (Romans 11:33)

America is clearly divided, over who we are as a nation. Some are so disillusioned, or misinformed, they would choose to rewrite our history, judging, condemning, and distorting reality. God has no problem with history. *"The eyes of the Lord are in every place, keeping watch on the evil and the good"* (Proverbs 15:3)

God's eyes have not been deceived. He knows the sins of slavery, and the decimation of the American Indian culture; permanent are those stains in the fabric of Old Glory. His eyes have also seen the bravery, courage, compassion, generosity, love, and forgiveness that have made America great among the nations. God knows the Truth. None are righteous, even in America.

So complete is God's knowledge that He knows every detail of our lives. He created us; we can have no secrets from Him. Our every thought, word, and habit are familiar to Him. *"You have searched me, LORD, and you know me. You know when I sit and when I rise; you perceive my thoughts from afar. You discern my going out and my lying down; you are familiar with all my ways. Before a word is on my tongue you, LORD, know it completely."* (Psalm 139:1-4)

Christian's take God's knowledge of them seriously. God is not to be mocked; however, personally, I think God must have a terrific sense of humor. We have the capacity to find humor in the human condition and laugh at our foolishness. It seems reasonable that the One who created us has an even greater sense of comedy. So, God has a serious nature that we dare not disrespect, but at the same time, He loves us, can laugh with us, and most importantly God knows our pain. *"The LORD looks from heaven; He sees all the sons of men. From the place of His dwelling He looks on all the inhabitants of the earth; He fashions their hearts individually; He considers all their works."* (Psalm 33:13-15)

God's knowledge penetrates the human heart. *"For this is what the high and exalted One says—He who lives forever, whose name is holy: 'I live in a high and holy place, but also with the one who is contrite and lowly in spirit, to revive the spirit of the lowly and to revive the heart of the contrite.'"* (Isaiah 57:15) To be contrite is to be ashamed, regretful, or grief-stricken. God loves us, understands us, and in those times when we're hurting, we can turn to Him. He will come close to us and revive our spirit.

God knows the future. He spoke to the prophets revealing things about His own nature and things yet to come, even Jesus prophesized about the signs and dangerous times marking his return to earth and warned us to be ready because no one knows when that time will come. *"Therefore, keep watch, because you do not know on what day your Lord will come. But understand this: If the owner of the house had known at what time of night the thief was coming, he would have kept watch and would not have let his house be broken into. So, you also must be ready, because the Son of Man will come at an hour when you do not expect him."* (Matthew 24: 42-44)

God is righteous. God's word defines all Truth and morality God's word is the standard for righteous behavior and judgment. Wise men enact only just laws that are aligned with the wisdom of the One who has created all things. His commandments encourage moral conduct leading to righteousness and virtue. They aren't meant to keep people from enjoying all that has been made, but indeed, they are essential to joy and happiness. In the absence of morality, disobedience reigns.

Outlaw groups like Al Qaeda, the Islamic State, and Boko Haram serve as examples of the terror that rains down on all when men turn their backs to the Creator. Uninhibited by God's commandments, they are more than willing to rape, pillage, and slaughter those who disagree with their version of truth. God defends those who pursue His righteous purpose. *"I will send my terror ahead of you and throw into confusion every nation you encounter. I will make all your enemies turn their backs and run."* (Exodus 23:27)

Yes, these are words He spoke to the Israelites, but under the new covenant, this promise would apply not just to the Jews, but to any Christian nation. *"If we confess our sins, he is faithful and just and will forgive us our sins and purify us from all unrighteousness."* (1 John 9:1)

God is omnipresent. Regardless of where we travel in this life, God is present. *"Yea, though I walk through the valley of the shadow of death, I will fear no evil, for thou are with me; your rod and thy staff, they comfort me."* (Psalms 23:4) Christians find great comfort in this verse. It's reassuring to know that even when confronted with evil, loneliness, doubt, grief, or persecution, that God's presence surrounds us.

"Where can I go from your Spirit? Where can I flee from your presence? If I go up to the heavens, you are there; if I make my bed in the depths, you are there. If I rise on the wings of the dawn, if I settle on the far side of the sea, even there your hand will guide me, your right hand will hold me fast." (Psalm 139:1-10)

Most Christians will tell you that it is in those quiet times, usually alone, perhaps in the fog on a lonely stretch of beach, or amid the silence of the forest, or beside the warmth of a fire on a cold winter's night, when we are most aware of The Divine Presence. *"Be still, and know that I am God…"* (Psalm 46:10)

"Fear not, for I am with you; be not dismayed, for I am your God; I will strengthen you; I will help you; and, I will uphold you with the right hand of my righteousness. (Isaiah 41:10) From the foxholes of a battlefield, amidst a raging hurricane, or learning the cancer is inoperable, we can lean on the promise of God that He will be with us always.

God renews and protects us. *"And be not conformed to this world: but be transformed by the renewing of your mind, that you may prove what is that good, and acceptable, and perfect, will of God."* (Romans 12:2) It does us no good to get caught up in the never-ending misdeeds of our fellow man, allowing them to destroy our peace of mind. We know that by renewing our thoughts, by turning our attention to the word of God, is how we protect ourselves from the shrillness, lies, and ugliness of the world.

As disciples of Christ, we have God's promise that we are, always, supplied with all that we need, and are surrounded by his presence, never to be forsaken. *"…Observe all things that I have commanded you; and lo, I am with you always, even to the end of the age.'"* (Matthew 28:20)

Not only in His word shall we find relief and renewal, but in His works. He gives us but a glimpse of heaven, but it stirs our souls. We are without excuse.

"The heavens declare the glory of God; and the firmament shows His handiwork. Day unto day utters speech, and night unto night reveals knowledge. There is no speech nor language, where their voice is not heard. Their line has gone out through all the earth, and their words to the end of the world." (Psalm 19:1-4)

Once we become disciples, we belong to Him, and cannot be taken from Him. We have His promise that we will be surrounded by His eternal protection against the forces of evil. *"And I give them eternal life, and they shall never perish; neither shall anyone snatch them out of my hand."* (John 10:28)

I believe God watches over us on this earth. Over the years, I've had more than my share of close calls, circumstances in which I probably should have been killed, but miraculously, was spared. I've heard others testify to God's mercy in situations when they confronted death face-to-face yet lived to tell about it. I'm convinced that he saves us for His purpose.

No one can explain or predict when such things will occur, but they do happen, and the beneficiary is left to ask, Why me Lord? Why have you spared me? *"For He shall give His angels charge over you, to keep you in all your ways. In their hands they shall bear you up, lest you dash your foot against a stone."* (Psalm 19:2)

God is forgiving. Not only does God forgives us, but He has given us the capacity to forgive. In those situations when we become angry, disappointed, forsaken, abused, or taken advantage of, God calls us to forgive. *"Let all bitterness, wrath, anger, clamor, and evil speaking be put away from you, with all malice. And be kind to one another, tenderhearted, forgiving one another, even as God in Christ forgave you."* (Ephesians 4: 31-32)

It is in this spirit that God has given us the power to overcome the human instinct to lash out, strike back, get revenge, punish, those who disrespect us, or mean to bring us harm. *"But if you do not forgive men their trespasses, neither will your Father forgive your trespasses."* (Matthew 6:15)

It is in our power to forgive, that we can overcome anger, prejudice, hate, to love the unlovable, and pray for our enemies. But, as in all aspects of our lives, God has given us free will; we can choose to forgive, or not. In Matthew 10:5-8, Jesus is instructing his disciples to go, not the way of Gentiles, or to the Samaritans, but to the lost sheep of Israel. Ending his instructions, he said, *"Freely you have received, freely give."*

We are so quick to forgive ourselves; difficult as it is, we should freely extend the same to others, lest we destroy ourselves. Before we judge, label, and condemn others, without even having listened to them, we would do well to remember our own faults; none are perfect. The increasing rancor in our nation is driving us apart. To paraphrase the words of St. Francis of Assisi, seek first to understand before being understood.

Don't misunderstand! Forgiveness doesn't mean we forget. God forgets. *"So great is His mercy toward those who fear Him. As far as the east is from the west, so far has He removed our transgressions."* (Psalm 103:11-12)

"For I will be merciful to their unrighteousness, and their sins and their lawless deeds I will remember no more." (Hebrews 8:12)

Notice, God forgets the transgressions of those who fear Him. Without repentance, there can be no forgiveness. We live in a world filled with evil. To forgive is divine. Forgiveness is at the very heart of the Christian faith.

On June 27, 2015, Dylan Roof, entered the historic Emanuel A.M.E. Church in Charleston, SC. Worshippers had gathered for Bible study led by the Rev. Clementa C. Pinckney. He invited the young white man to join them. As the study was ending, Roof who had come armed, stood and began shooting. Nine worshippers, including Pinckney, were murdered in cold blood.

In court, Roof showed no remorse, said nothing was wrong with him psychologically, and his purpose was to start a race war. Evil, pure and simple. But, with the power to forgive, many survivors and relatives of the martyrs, told Roof that their faith had called them to forgive him, and to pray for him, asking God's mercy on his soul.

Bethane Middleton-Brown, sister of the slain Rev. DePayne Middleton-Doctor, said to Roof, "I wanted to hate you, but my faith tells me no. I wanted to remain angry, but my view of life won't let me. You took someone precious from me, but my faith tells me she was a borrowed angel God called home. You can't look at me, but when you're alone you will hear my voice and see my face."

Later, it was observed that with the outpouring of prayer, sympathy, and support of the Charleston community, South Carolina, and the nation, that Roof's hatred was quickly turned in to love. Rather than starting a race war, he united all people of good faith to stand together in the knowledge that love overcomes hate. We can forgive. To do otherwise will destroy us, but because we live in an evil world, we shall not forget.
(https://abcnews.go.com/US/charleston-victims-mother-tells-dylann-roof-forgive)

America would benefit greatly if we could remember: Good neighbors can disagree without being disagreeable. *"To err is human; to forgive, divine."* Alexander Pope (An essay on criticism, 1711)

Then Jesus said, "Father, forgive them, for they know not what they do." And they divided His garments and cast lots. (Luke 23:34)

LDS Photo Library:soldierscastinglots/jesus

God is omnipotent. He is all-powerful. *"The LORD has established his throne in heaven, and his kingdom rules over all."* (Psalm 103:19) If it serves His purpose, all things are possible. Christians believe God is in control now and forever. That is an accepted fact, just as many unbelievers consider Darwinian evolution to be a fact. Neither side's disbelief will change the "facts" accepted by the opposing side. Let's examine the beliefs of humanists.

God has emotions. *Then God said, 'Let Us make man in Our image, according to Our likeness; let them have dominion over the fish of the sea, over the birds of the air, and over the cattle, over all the earth and over every creeping thing that creeps on the earth.'"* (Genesis 1:26)

It would seem logical that because God created mankind in His image, giving us certain characteristics, they would somewhat resemble His. Having endowed us with traits that are akin to His, allows us to build a relationship with Him. Without benefit of some common qualities, there could be no mutual understanding, no communication of emotions related to love, sorrow, joy, thanksgiving, and forgiveness.

"There is a season, a time for every purpose under heaven. ... A time to weep, and a time to laugh; a time to mourn, and a time to dance." (Ecclesiastes 1,4)

Our emotions are one of our most precious gifts from God. Can you even begin to imagine what humanity would look like without the capacity to express the broad range of feelings that sets us apart from his other creations?

"What is man, that you are mindful of him? and the son of man, that you care for him?" (Psalms 8:4)

Deep within the human brain, the Creator has placed a fail/safe mechanism, we call the limbic system. It's located at the top of the brain stem and is responsible for emotions, survival instincts, and memory. The Creator designed this system to process information essential to our safety and well-being. Intuitively, we sense situations that threaten our safety and all systems are put on notice—fight or run! Most creatures are gifted with this warning signal.

God has blessed humans with additional sensory processors; among them are the amygdalae, two almond size organs, one on each side of the head near the ears. They respond to signals that trigger emotions at a higher level than animal instinct. Oxford University scientists recently discovered that the prefrontal cortex has a uniquely human function. Researchers believe the lateral frontal pole receives information from other primary systems (Limbic

& cerebellum) and responds in a variety of ways, including planning, decision making, and the ability to rethink things and change our minds. These qualities clearly set humans apart from all other species. (http://www.ox.ac.uk/news/2014-01-28-brain-area-unique-humans-linked-cognitive-powers)

The evolutionists might want to reconsider how many eons it would take for a system of conscious thought to evolve that enables humans to "see" another person's point of view, evaluate it, consider other options, and examine its moral and ethical implications, all within split seconds. We serve an amazing God!

Without doubt, God has expressed love, compassion, and forgiveness; these are well known to anyone who has heard the Gospel message. His wrath is also well known, but often misunderstood. It's an attribute that causes some people to turn away, thinking of Him as mean-spirited and threatening. *"You shall not follow other gods, any of the gods of the peoples who surround you, for the LORD your God in the midst of you is a jealous God; otherwise, the anger of the LORD your God will be kindled against you, and He will wipe you from the face of the earth."* (Deuteronomy 16: 4-15)

These are strong words indeed. God is angry. God is jealous. God speaks in a wrathful tone. But, is His warning mean-spirited and threatening? Christians refer to God as our Father in heaven. God loves us as any father should love his children. He wants the best for us. Responsible, loving fathers are required to guide and direct their children toward successful, fulfilling lives, keeping them away from harm and disappointment. *"Thou art worthy, O Lord, to receive glory and honor and power: for thou hast created all things, and for thy pleasure they are and were created."* (Revelation 4:11)

"So, God created man in his [own] image, in the image of God created he him; male and female created he them." (Genesis 1:27)

"This people have I formed for myself; they shall show forth my praise." (Isaiah 43:21)

These verses confirm that God created us for his own purpose and pleasure. He surely wants to enjoy the fruits of his creation. So why is He jealous and angry? Like any loving father, He doesn't want his children focusing on things that are not in their best interest. Therefore, God wants us to stay sharply focused on Him, not on money, lust, booze, drugs, power, and "stuff." Worshipping at the altar of material things and temptations of this world will lead to a world of pain and disappointment. He is jealous of things that interfere with our reliance on his instructions for joyful living. God wants us to enjoy all of creation. He takes pleasure in our joy.

God unleashes his wrath There are two examples of God passing judgment on people who had drifted so deeply into wickedness and immorality that He was compelled to wipe them from the earth. The generation of Noah was so overcome with sexual perversion, corruption, and Satanic influence, that God declared the people spiritually dead. He instructed Noah—120 years in advance—to build an ark to save himself, his family, and pairs of animals from a flood that would destroy all life on earth. Noah faithfully told the people why he was building the ark. They laughed and called him a fool. They had plenty of time to repent; they did not. The rain came. They knocked at the doors begging to come aboard. It was too late. (Genesis 6:9, 8:2)

The second example is found in Genesis 19. It describes the complete destruction of the cities of Sodom and Gomorrah and the surrounding plain. One day, three men came to visit Abraham, a Jewish patriarch, after having a meal with him, one of the men spoke. *"The outcry against Sodom and Gomorrah is so great and their sin so grievous that I will go down and see if what they have done is as bad as the outcry that has reached me. If not, I will know."*

Two of the men left to travel to Sodom. Abraham stood before the man that had spoken and recognized him as LORD. Abraham's nephew, Lot and his family were living near Sodom. *"Will you sweep away the righteous with the wicked? What if there are fifty righteous people in the city? Will you really sweep it away? ... Far be it from you to do such a thing—to kill the righteous with the wicked ... Will not the Judge of all the earth do right?"*

The LORD and Abraham debated the number of righteous people it would take for the city to be spared. Abraham continued to boldly negotiate for his nephew Lot, his family, and any righteous people to be found. Finally, the LORD agreed, *"For the sake of ten, I will not destroy it.* Lot and his family were led to safety before the cities were destroyed by fire and brimstone raining down from the heavens. (See Genesis 18:1-33)

God is not to be mocked. It grieves God, as it does any father, to severely punish children who cross the line without remorse. We've reached a point in America where there are people who appear to be above the law, avoiding the penalty they deserve. Punishment and accountability are partners. The result of one without the other is likely to be injustice.

The wrath of God eventually falls on the godless and wicked who ignore Truth. Since the creation of the universe, God has made it plain for all to see. His invisible qualities, eternal power, and divine nature have been clearly seen, by what has been made plain, so people are without excuse. Because they deny and disrespect the knowledge of God, He will, at some point, give 'em what they want, free to do whatever in the name of self-determination. (See Romans 1:18-32)

God doesn't condemn us to hell. When we fail to acknowledge his power and authority, we condemn ourselves.

Wake up America. God is who He says He is! His patience and forbearance are great, but not without limits. *"The LORD could no longer bear your evil deeds and the abominations that you committed. Therefore, your land has become a desolation and a waste and a curse, without inhabitant, as it is this day."* (Jeremiah 44:22)

The prophet, Jeremiah, is mourning the destruction that God had wrought upon the people of Judah because they had forsaken Him pursuing a pagan lifestyle, worshipping false gods, including the sacrifice of infants. God had spoken many times, warning the people through the words of the prophet that if they didn't repent and turn their hearts back toward Him, they would face severe punishment for their lies, adultery, drunkenness, and other evil practices, violating the covenant God had established with their forefathers.

The people didn't listen, paid no attention to the warnings given again and again. Jeremiah was mocked, beaten, imprisoned, but he was steadfast in his calling.

In 605 B. C., Nebuchadnezzar, King of Babylon began a series of attacks on Judah, eventually taking control of the country. In 587, the Babylonians destroyed Jerusalem, burned King Solomon's Temple to the ground, killed the elite military guard, and took thousands captive.

Infanticide, drugs, drunkenness, adultery, lying, sexual immorality, turning away from God, worshipping false gods—America looks a lot like Judah 600 B.C. Hey, what's to worry? No God. No Problem!

The Religious Human Manifesto III (2003) makes two points that clearly reveal the schism between their beliefs and those of Christianity.

Life's fulfillment emerges from individual participation in the service of humane ideals. We aim for our fullest possible development and animate our lives with a deep sense of purpose, finding wonder and awe in the joys and beauties of human existence, its challenges and tragedies, and even in the inevitability and finality of death. Humanists rely on the rich heritage of human culture and the life-stance of Humanism to provide comfort in times of want and encouragement in times of plenty.

Humans are an integral part of nature, the result of unguided evolutionary change. Humanists recognize nature as self-existing. We accept our life as all and enough, distinguishing things as they are from things as we might wish or imagine them to be. We welcome the challenges of the future and are drawn to and undaunted by the yet to be known." (https://americanhumanist.org/what-is-humanism/manifesto3/)

These statements in part explain the fundamental philosophy and appeal of the *American Humanist Association – Good without God*. I understand its appeal—

humane, progressive, without supernaturalism, affirming, responsible, intelligible, ethical, fulfilling, aspirational, all for the greater good.

I never thought of myself as a "humanist," but my worldview certainly aligned with that philosophy. I recall that in the seventies, secular humanism had taken root in our school corporation. A few parents expressed concern that it would creep into our classrooms. I read the pamphlet they left with me. That evening, I read it to my graduate class, mostly teachers, aspiring to become school administrators. In my naivete, I said something about it didn't sound so threatening to me. It asks that a man stand on his own two feet, be discerning, live by the Golden Rule, take care of business in a moral and ethical manner etc., What's wrong with that?

After class was over, one young man remained, obviously wanting to speak to me. It was odd because he wasn't one to speak out in class. I asked if he had a question. He answered saying he'd been thinking about my view of secular humanism. He went on, "Maybe the parents are afraid that because humanists don't believe in God, that their kids will be taught that God doesn't exist. There's a danger that people who want to live without God, to become their own little gods." He acknowledged the nod of my head. As he turned to go, he added, "I thought you might like to know that." Obviously, I've never forgotten it. That's the flip side of the testimony given by atheists who say, "Yes, I've read the bible. That's why I'm an atheist."

Either God is all-powerful, or God does not exist. We get to choose freely. If we stand by our choice, we should extend respect one to the other. Integrity counts.

Who is Jesus?
God in Human Flesh

"In the beginning was the Word, and the Word was with God; and the Word was God." (John 1:1)

The Gospel of John tells us of the coming of Jesus and describes his divine nature. "The Word," translated from Hebrew, means the "power of God to create." From the Greek it refers to God's wisdom and the reasoning behind his creation. (http://www.ancient-hebrew.org/40_genesis1.html)

The first verse of the Gospel of John makes clear that The Word and God are one in the same and is reinforced in later verses. *"And the Word became flesh and dwelt among us."* (John 1:14)

There seems to be a tendency for people to think of the human nature of Jesus. We think of him as the baby in a manger, as a great teacher, and as a man persecuted and crucified for our sins. We might be tempted to simply say "ditto" to the characteristics of God Almighty and be done with this question of who is Jesus? Failing to acknowledge the uniqueness of Jesus would be a great injustice to his extraordinary role in the Trinity. There is but one Jesus and his characteristics are distinctly his. He didn't just come from Bethlehem. He came from the eternal, the infinite Son of God. The source of our salvation, after being crucified, he arose from the tomb and ascended into the heavens. Jesus is God. He appeared on earth to make known his divine nature to humankind. What evidence do we have that Jesus and God are one in the same?

If Jesus is not who he proclaims to be then Christianity is empty, without substance. As Paul said, *"If Christ has not been raised, our preaching is useless, and so is your faith, ... we are of all people most to be pitied."* (1 Corinthians: 15:12-19)

Let's use scripture, not opinion, to help answer the question: Is Jesus God? Christians believe:

Jesus is God. Some unbelievers, when debating the Truth of Jesus will point to the fact that the *Holy Bible* has not recorded a specific occasion when Jesus actually said, I am God. One reason might be that a man who says he's God is either delusional, a liar, or he understands that to make that claim was, in those times, considered a crime punishable by death by stoning. However, there are many occasions on record, when Jesus clearly identified himself as God.

Speaking before the Pharisees, Jesus was asked a question about his identity. *"Very truly I tell you,"* Jesus answered, *"before Abraham was born, I am!"* (John 8:58) Remember, Moses asked God who he should tell the people it was that had spoken to him? God replied in no uncertain terms, *"I AM WHO I AM. This is what you are to say to the Israelites: I AM has sent me.* The Pharisees immediately understood what Jesus was saying. A man, claiming, that *before Abraham, I am!"* He's saying he is God! Blasphemy! They were ready to stone him. In this statement, by affirming his eternal presence with God, Jesus affirms himself to be co-equal with God.

Jesus is the Son of God. During the Festival of Dedication, in Jerusalem, Jesus again was answering questions posed by the religious leaders. He replied that he had already answered their questions and they didn't believe him. He responded saying, *"You do not believe because you are not my sheep – my sheep listen to my voice. My Father, who has given them to me, is greater than all, no one can snatch them out of my Father's hand. I and the Father are one."* (John 10:29-30) Again, they gathered up stones ready to kill him, a mere man, claiming God to be his Father! In this statement, Jesus affirms himself to be the Son of God.

It makes no sense for a rational man to identify himself as God, when knowing that his enemies are eager for an opportunity to kill him. The unbelievers will likely say, exactly the point! He's not a rational man. There were those among the Jewish authorities who tried to write him off as "possessed by demons, a raving madman," There were others that disagreed, citing his works and teaching as signs of a knowledgeable man in full control of his words and actions. Those were the ones who rightly perceived him as a threat to their political power.

Just for good measure, there are other verses where Jesus is identified as one in the same with God. *"Keep watch over yourselves and all the flock of which the Holy Spirit has made you overseers. Be shepherds of the church of God, which he bought with his own blood."* (Acts 20:28) Clearly, Jesus is the one, that on the cross, shed his blood. The verse says God purchased the Church with "his own blood." We understand the blood was shed by one and the same. *"Believe me when I say that I am in the Father and the Father is in me."* (John 14:11)

Jesus is eternal, immortal. *"In the beginning was the Word – and the Word was God."* (John 1:1) Jesus was before time, before the earth and heavens were formed.

On the night of his arrest, prior to his crucifixion, Jesus was preparing the disciples for what was to come. In their presence he prayed, *"Father, the hour has come. Glorify your Son, that your Son may glorify you. — I have brought you glory on earth by finishing the work you gave me to do. And now, Father, glorify me in your presence with the glory I had with you before the world began."* (John 17: 1-5)

So, Jesus is before the beginning and then without end. *"And lo, I am with you always, even unto the end of the age."* (Matt. 28:20) *"I am the Alpha and the Omega, the First and the Last, the Beginning and the End."* (Revelation 22: 13) Also in Revelation 1: 17-18, is his testimony to immortality. *"Do not be afraid; I am the First and the Last. I am He who lives, and was dead, and behold, I am alive forevermore. Amen"* All who believe, find comfort in those words.

Jesus possesses all authority. God has extended to Jesus the power to make the final pronouncement in all matters. *"All authority has been given to Me in heaven and on earth."* (Matt. 28:18) *"All things have been committed to me by my father."* (Luke 10:22) Jesus' authority includes supernatural power to drive out demons and to overcome the physical laws of the universe.

During his brief ministry, Jesus performed dozens of miracles witnessed by people wherever he taught. He never performed miracles for "show nor dough." Each miracle had a message to communicate, a specific purpose to meet a person's need, or make a point regarding his identity.

For example, the first miracle mentioned in the Bible was turning water into wine. (John 2:1-11) In doing so, he revealed his power over physical elements. When he drove out demons from a man possessed by evil spirits, (Mark 1:21-27) witnesses were amazed that Jesus could rid one possessed of unclean spirits by commanding them to leave the man's body, a demonstration of his authority.

Jesus has authority to overcome whatever stands between him and righteousness. *"Behold, I give unto you power to tread on serpents and scorpions, and over all the power of the enemy: and nothing shall by any means hurt you."* (Luke 10:19)

He has the authority to forgive sins, judge all the nations and all of mankind, authority to grant eternal life, authority to receive the righteous into the Kingdom, the authority to condemn the unbelievers. *"Whoever believes in the Son, has eternal life, but whoever rejects the Son will not have life, for God's wrath remains on him."* (John 3:36)

If you have any doubt, consider this; God placed the sin of the world upon the shoulders of our Savior. Jesus was obedient, willing to pay for all of us, the sum of mankind's sin, because there was no way under the sun we could pay that price.

Wrath, in that day didn't mean anger, it meant a just and appropriate punishment for wickedness; therefore, God did not spare the Son the punishment we deserved. His wrath was squarely upon the Son. Jesus shed every drop of blood to take away the stain of sin, thereby restoring the bridge, the relationship, between God and man. Only Jesus had the authority to give his life, the authority to overcome death. *"But I want you to know that the Son of Man has authority on earth to forgive sins. So he (Jesus) said."* (Mark 2:10)

When dying on the cross at Golgotha, Jesus said, *"Father, forgive them, for they know not what they do."* One of the criminals being executed alongside him, acknowledged that unlike them, Jesus had committed no crime; then he said to Jesus, *"Lord, remember me when You come into Your kingdom."* Jesus replied, *"Assuredly, I say to you, today you will be with Me in Paradise."* (Luke 23: 42-43) It could be said that forgiveness is at the very heart of the Christian faith. Every Christian understands, if we do not forgive others, we shall not be forgiven.

Jesus can perform miracles. Two of the best-known miracles performed by Jesus are found in Matthew

<u>14</u>: beginning verse 13. Jesus was seeking some time to himself and had gone by boat to a solitary spot, but a large crowd had gathered there ahead of him, hoping to hear him preach. Having compassion on them he went about preaching and healing the sick.

As evening approached, the disciples suggested that the crowd be dispersed so they could go into nearby towns and get food. Jesus said the people didn't need to scatter. He told the disciples to feed them. They protested that there wasn't near enough food to satisfy such a large gathering, having only two fish and five loaves of bread.

Jesus directed the people to sit down in the grass. Taking the loaves and the two fish and looking up to heaven, he gave thanks, broke the loaves and gave them to the disciples, who, in turn passed them among the crowd. About five thousand men, and in addition, women and children ate and were satisfied. Following the meal, the disciples picked up twelve basketfuls of broken pieces left over. This was not a magic trick done for pleasure. It was done to reveal his divine nature to as many followers as possible.

<u>Matthew</u>, verse 22, begins with the disciples boarding a boat to return to the other side of the lake; Jesus was going to walk and engage in prayer time, planning to meet them on the other side. The wind was very strong; the disciples were unable to control the boat and it was blown far from shore. Just before dawn, Jesus went out to them, walking on the surface of Galilee.

He appeared to them unexpectedly; in the early morning mist, they were terrified thinking it was a ghost. Jesus called out reassuring them not to be afraid. *"Lord, if it's you,"* Peter replied, *"call me to come to you on the water."* Jesus motioned to him. *"Come,"* he said.

Peter stepped out of the boat and walked on the water toward Jesus. But when he encountered the fierce wind, he was afraid and, beginning to sink, he called out, *"Lord, save me!"* Jesus reached out his hand and caught him. Then he issued a statement familiar to nearly everyone. *"O' Ye of little faith,"* he said, *"why did you doubt?"* How many times have I stumbled like Peter?

Jesus and Peter climbed into the boat, the wind died down. Those in the boat understood they had witnessed the supernatural and worshiped him, saying, *"Truly you are the Son of God."* (Matthew 14:33) Miracles have a purpose.

The supernatural power that Christ has is among the issues that aggravate unbelievers. It simply drives them up the wall that any reasonable person would believe such nonsense, walking on water, feeding five thousand people with five loaves of stale bread and two dead fish. Their pride and their intellect won't allow it. It would be too embarrassing to have other rational people discover that they believe in myths and fairy tales, rather than the reality of modern science. I can understand that.

"You don't have enough faith," Jesus told them. "I tell you the truth, if you had faith even as small as a mustard seed, you could say to this mountain, 'Move from here to there,' and it would move. Nothing would be impossible to you." (Matthew 17:20)

"For no one who performs a miracle in My name can soon afterward speak evil of Me." (Mark 9:39)

Some unbelievers struggle with the fact that Jesus has warned Christians not to demonstrate their faith, or test his promise, by jumping from a twelve-story building and landing safely. They see it as a cop-out; saying Jesus doesn't have the power to do that. I come back to the examples above. Such powers are to be used with discretion. Jesus is not with Ringling Brothers. He exercises his supernatural influence according to his time, place, and purpose. There are people living today, who will testify that they would not be here, had they not been spared by a life-saving a miracle of Christ.

Jesus is/was without sin. The only one not defiled by sin was Jesus; therefore, it was his life, and his only, that could make atonement for our sinful nature. The wages of sin is death; it's that simple. Sin cannot be allowed to enter heaven. God's kingdom is free from sin. If we have any hope of life after death, we must be free of sin. Jesus has paid our way to make that possible.

I'm a simple man; I can understand atonement like this. Let's say I'm a young married man with two young children and a startup business venture, I make a bad decision and knowingly break the law. My crime is brought to light. I'm arrested. An older man had shown faith in me and helped me get started in business. He comes to visit me in the local jail. I'm deeply remorseful, regretful that I had chosen to deceive, and in so doing, embarrassed my entire family, friends, and greatly disappointed him.

He believes I've been truly humbled by my shameful act putting my family and the fledgling business at risk. He antes up the bail money. I'm released to rejoin my family until the trial.

I plead guilty as charged. My mentor vouches for me, telling the judge that he and a partner will continue to walk alongside me as advisors. The judge foregoes jail time, sentencing me to pay a $25,000.00 fine as reparation for my offense. There's absolutely no way I can come up with that amount—the debt is too great. My mentor understands. If I'm not too proud to accept his offer, he's ready to pay my debt in full, atonement for my stupidity and allowing me a second chance. I can't repay in full, but I can reward his faith by leading the life he modeled for me.

Jesus can overcome death. The suffering of Jesus on the cross, bearing the sin of all of humanity, ended as he spoke these words, *"It is finished,"* and with that last breath, gave up his spirit. He had been obedient to his Father's will, accomplishing what he had been sent to do—restore the relationship between God and His people.

Pastor Josh McDowell, (*Evidence That Demands a Verdict*, Publisher: Blackstone Audio Inc., 2017) explains that Jesus sacrificed his life for you, me, all of humanity to remove the stain of our sinful nature. We understand that it is God's nature to be holy, righteous, and just. To enter an intimate relationship with the God of all creation, we must be without sin. It's impossible that any of us can accomplish atonement for sin on our own. Only the blood of Christ could satisfy that condition.

Following his crucifixion, Jesus' body had been removed from the cross. Joseph of Arimathea, and Nicodemus, received permission from Pontius Pilate, governor of Judea, to take the body and prepare it for burial. There was a garden nearby in which was a tomb that had only been recently opened. Jesus' body was treated with spices, wrapped in strips of linen, and laid in the tomb. Roman soldiers rolled a heavy stone into place to seal it, then stood by to keep watch as they had been assigned.

At daybreak on the third day following Jesus' death, Mary Magdalene, Mary, mother of James, and some other women, went to visit the tomb. The stone had been rolled away; there were no guards. They entered the tomb and found it was empty. Only the linen strips remained, and the cloth that had been wrapped around his head was folded neatly in a place by itself. Confused by what they had seen, they came out of the tomb, and found two men dressed in snow-white garments. Now, they were frightened and bowed down in submission. One of the men asked, *"Why seek ye the living among the dead?* The other said, *"He is not here, but risen. Remember what he told you when in Galilee, saying the Son of Man must be delivered into the hands of sinful men and be crucified, and the third day rise again."* (Luke 24:5-6)

The women ran to tell the apostles what they had seen. In disbelief, Peter ran to the tomb and confirmed what he had been told. In the evening of that same day, the apostles had gathered together to discuss what had happened. As he had promised, but still, to their surprise, Jesus returned to instruct them in how to go about the business of spreading the good news, that he had conquered the grave.

In his glorified form, he came through the locked doors where the disciples were gathered, all but Thomas, who for unknown reasons wasn't present. Jesus breathed the Holy Spirit upon them and explained the powers and authority that they would be given to continue his work on earth.

A week thereafter, all came together again; Thomas is with them. The others told him about their first encounter with the Risen Christ. (Thomas and I must have something in common, that of being doubtful. Maybe we both have relatives in Missouri, the Show Me State! In 1899, Rep. Willard D. Vandiver said, "Frothy eloquence neither convinces nor satisfies me. I'm from Missouri. You've got to show me!) I share Vandiver's skepticism, especially in our age of 24/7/365 "breaking news," and misrepresentations on social media. So be it.

Thomas replied to them, *"Unless I see the mark of the nails in his hands and put my finger into the nail marks and put my hand into his side, I will not believe."* (John 20:25)

Again, as at the first meeting, the doors were locked. Jesus suddenly appears to them. *"Peace be with you,"* he said; then turning toward Thomas, he said, *"Put your finger here and see my hands, and bring your hand and put it into my side, and do not be unbelieving, but believe." Thomas answered and said to him, "My Lord and my God!"* (John 20:24-28)

Earlier I confessed I sometimes find myself doubting God's promises, then something happens, and I say to myself, "O' ye of little faith." The same is true of doubt. This world is so full of lies and deception, sorry, but I believe only the most innocent, or naïve, would have much trust in anything these days. I surely can't be alone in my cynicism, and that's why, in these days of chaos, gross exaggeration, and unabashed hypocrisy, I find myself trusting only in the Truth of God.

Unbelievers have only the opinions and the knowledge of other humans upon which they form their own opinions and knowledge. Surely, one must pick and choose, a little of this, a little of that, and what kind of truth is the result? I've chosen the eternal Truth. Thomas, Doubting Thomas, wanted to be shown the Truth. He understood that those accepting the job of taking the Gospel message into an unbelieving world would be persecuted, perhaps killed. Thomas was no fool; he loved Jesus, but wanted assurance, he wasn't risking his life for a lie.

Then Jesus told him (Thomas), *"Because you have seen me, you have believed; blessed are those who have not seen and yet have believed."* (John 20:29)

I can identify with Thomas. I find it curious that he wasn't present at the first meeting. Christians believe there is no "luck;" all things have a purpose. This doesn't equate to predestination, we're not puppets on a string, or robots moving only in response to the operator's controls. It simply acknowledges that God can take anything, even evil, and turn it to His purpose and to our benefit. So, when Thomas shows up at the second meeting, Jesus confronts him regarding his disbelief.

"Here," Jesus says, *"Put your finger here and see my hands, and bring your hand and put it into my side."* I find it curious that Jesus didn't chastise Thomas for his doubt. Jesus is not one to mince words; therefore, he must have had compassion for Thomas, an intelligent, loyal follower, but one needing a little support at crunch time. Come, I think Jesus was saying. Come, Thomas, feel these wounds, see these scars, you can believe in them.

I find it more than curious, that as I read this and understand what has been written, I am struck with the feeling that Thomas has done for me what I can't do for myself. It wasn't by accident that Thomas was absent from the first meeting. At the second meeting, because he doubted, he was invited to touch. He touched. He saw. He believed. His faith was reinforced, fulfilled.

Jesus said, *"Because you have seen me, you have believed; blessed are those who have not seen and yet have believed."* I have not touched; I have not seen, there are times when I have doubts, but because of Thomas, I take comfort and assurance in Jesus' words, *blessed are those who have not seen and yet have believed."* It is said

Thomas died at the hands of religious leaders, in India or Greece, run through by a spear. Was he martyred for a lie?

No. Thomas died for the Truth. Jesus is God as He appears to mankind on earth. He will come again.

The Holy Bible tells us Christ will return to claim His Church. No one knows when that time will come. Will you be ready? Have you made Jesus the Lord of your life?

If you're already a believer, what is your loyalty to Christ worth to you? What are you willing to risk for Him?

What are you doing to fulfill his command to go forth and make disciples for God's glory?

Have you forgiven those who have trespassed against you?

At some point in our lives, these questions must be addressed. Ignoring them is the same as answering them in the negative.

Dr. Francis Schaeffer

America the Beautiful
Taken Captive by the Lie

There are many things we could agree on that make our country great, but one of the great things about America is that Americans are forever protesting, disagreeing, and complaining about all manner of things, It's the American way. Individual liberty, freedom to speak, and to act, protected by laws, guaranteed by the blood of patriots; for more than two and half centuries, we have enjoyed these blessings. Sadly, some of us are now mistaking them for entitlements, a dangerous mindset. Getting things for free, is a subtle lie, that too many people buy into, not realizing what they have compromised in the process.

Dictionary definitions define a lie as deceptive words or actions intended to mislead others, to the benefit of the individual or group spreading the falsehood. Because we're gullible and self-serving, lies get passed along by those who are simply naïve, and by those who think they will benefit from the lie.

It is not considered a lie if a group or individual, in good faith, communicate certain "facts" that later turn out to be false. Liars are those who know the truth but, hide it intentionally. Knowledge is power, the power to control the minds and actions of the ignorant – that is to say, those who lack knowledge. Let's examine six lies that divide and continue to weaken the moral and ethical fabric of America.

Part Two

Six Lies:

That Changed America

"Woe to the world because of its stumbling blocks! For it is inevitable that stumbling block come; but woe to that man through whom the stumbling block comes!" (Matthew 18:7-9)

1859 - Charles Darwin: *Children of God or the Goo?*

1952 - Hugh Hefner: *The Playboy Culture*

1963 - Madalyn Murray O'Hair: *God Expelled from School*

1971 - The Pentagon Papers: *Lies Revealed*

1973 - Roe v. Wade: *Abortion on Demand*

2015 – Sphere Sovereignty: *Trashing Individual Rights*

1859 - Charles Darwin:
Children of God or the Goo?

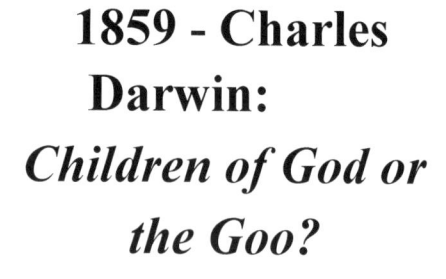

In 1859, the bible of evolution, *On the Origin of Species*, by Charles Darwin was published.

In 1831, Darwin, then a graduate of Cambridge, was a young and inexperienced naturalist; however, he received an invitation to join a team of British scientists on a voyage around the world to study how changes in weather, food sources, and geological habitat impacted the life cycles of various species of mammals, birds, and fish. Following his five-year voyage aboard the HMS Beagle, he began drawing from the data that had been compiled, writing articles for science journals and monographs, sharing his observations with other professionals.

He noted that some species, when confronted with significant changes in their environment, that altered or threatened their survival, were able to make slight modifications in their habits and physical appearance. Those species, he believed, were able to "evolve" to a higher level of behavior, avoiding extinction by passing the adaptation on to successive generations. Those that failed to adapt, died out. It was a theory based on natural selection, but commonly known as "survival of the fittest." (A phrase coined by Herbert Spencer, Atheist, 1859)

Darwin hypothesized that these slight changes over time, eons of time, could explain how species were able to evolve, one slight change at a time, each change leading to a more sophisticated, complex creature. His explanations caught the attention of not only the scientific community, but educators, and the public at large.

Ironically, Darwin was surprised at how quickly and enthusiastically his hypothesis was accepted. He identified potential gaps in his work, saying that fossilized plants and creatures would have to reveal a record of the thousands of transitional phases required to change one life form into a new one. The fossil record to date shows no such evidence. To his credit, he also noted:

> "If it could be demonstrated that any complex organ existed which could not possibly have been formed by numerous, successive, slight modifications, my theory would absolutely break down."

In 1859, there were no electron microscopes with the capacity to enlarge images of specimens by 50 million times in 3-D. A diagram in my biology text in 1954, consists of a cell wall containing a nucleus, cytoplasm, and vacuole. We had no idea!

Modern technology has destroyed Darwin's theory. Michael J. Katz, *Templets and the Explanation of Complex Patterns* (Cambridge University Press, 1986) writes:

> "In the natural world, there are many pattern-assembly systems...there are useful scientific explanations for these complex systems, but final patterns...are so heterogeneous...they cannot

effectively be reduced to smaller…less intricate components…I will argue these patterns are, in a fundamental sense, irreducibly complex."

I interpret this to mean that any organism, even a single cell, is complex, configured in predetermined patterns (DNA/RNA); therefore, it cannot assemble itself spontaneously. If the templet is not present, the organism cannot form. Life cannot form itself in the absence of a preexisting set of instructions.

Furthermore, Katz says Darwin's idea that a random event, that introduces a new element in the structure of the species, will result in an improved variety, has been shown through numerous experiments to be false. On the contrary, random alterations in the templet (DNA), will result in deformities, sometimes grotesque, hampering the organism's ability to function. Thus, it devolves, rather than evolves! New technology has shown Darwin's work to be erroneous. R.I.P.

Charles Darwin 1809-1892

Photo by Maull & PollyBlank/1855/wikipedia

Every lie has consequences. Every disagreement has at least two sides. Did Darwin lie, or were his motives misunderstood? This remains controversial; however, even his supporters acknowledge, that he clearly saw the potential of his work to challenge century old beliefs regarding creation, and to undermine the authority of the Church. Letters from his wife, Emma, suggest that his theory of natural selection was troublesome, and in conflict with her Christian faith.

Darwin chose to perpetuate research that he clearly knew was incomplete, barely solid enough to label his work a hypothesis. That his work was given the distinction of being accepted as a theory was taxing to biologists and other scientists, who pointed to the gaps, the broad assumptions, and extrapolation required to give scientific credence to his body of work.

Furthermore, because of the damage his work has done around the world, over the past century and a half, it was unfortunate that Darwin's writings became popular so fast. The unbelievers had been handed "scientific evidence," facts, to justify their denial of God. They took every opportunity to erase God and religion from every aspect of society, something our Forefathers warned about.

> *"The only foundation for . . . a republic is to be laid in Religion. Without this there can be no virtue, and without virtue there can be no liberty, and liberty is the object and life of all republican governments.*
>
> *'Benjamin Rush (1745-1813) American Patriot*

The Spread of Darwinism:
Social Consequences

Worldwide, the social consequences of Darwinism have resulted in a horrific toll of human suffering at the hands of monsters such as Adolph Hitler, Pol Pot, and Joseph Stalin. If one believes that humans are nothing more than higher order animals, having evolved through the process of natural selection, and that the weak must die, so that the strong may flourish, then it becomes the duty of those in charge to ensure the prosperity of the strong.

These three men exemplify what happens when God is removed from the social order. Collectively, they are directly responsible for the deaths of a loosely estimated 36 million human beings. Children, women, and men, tortured, starved, beaten, shot, beheaded, gassed, burned, drowned, why, we ask? Why!?

Adolph Hitler was Reich Chancellor of Germany's, Nazi Party, 1933-1945. Hitler's worldview included not only universal domination, but ethnic cleansing as well. He fully believed Darwin's theory, that within the order of species, some are superior. It became his dream to create a "master" race, the Aryan race (noble, eminent, elevated among men), ultimately, a race of "supermen."

It has been estimated that between 12-14 million died as a direct result of Hitler's reign of terror designed to eradicate Gypsies, Poles, and Jews—"dregs of humanity."

Joseph Stalin was Premier of the Soviet Union, Communist Party from 1922-1952. Estimates vary widely, but the median figure would suggest that 20 million

Russian citizens, and political enemies, died at his hands. It can't be said Darwinism was the sole driving force behind the brutal, iron-fisted, unforgiving practices of Stalin. It was politics, economics, military might, and religion that combined in a deadly mix for those living through those times; but, surely Stalin didn't miss the point. If there is no God, he's irrelevant. Don't worry, just do as you like. Might makes right!

Pol Pot was Leader of the Khmer Rouge, Cambodia (Democratic Kampuchea) from 1975-1985. The following serves as an example of what can happen when Darwinism takes root in the mind of an unstable dictator. In 1978, Cambodia was at war with Vietnam. In May, of that year, Cambodian socialists rebelled in the eastern part of the country. Pol Pot issued a radio broadcast threatening to exterminate 50 million Vietnamese, and "purify" the masses of Cambodia. He was preparing to exterminate his own citizens that he branded as "Khmer bodies with Vietnamese minds." In six months, more than 100,000 "undesirables" were slaughtered in the "killing fields" of Cambodia. (https://en.wikipedia.org/wiki/Pol_Pot)

Pol Pot's wickedness ended when the Army of Vietnam drove him into hiding. He committed suicide, thus ending his threat to execute 50 million more Vietnamese. Altogether, an estimated 2 million Cambodians and Vietnamese were murdered by one who felt justified in applying the law of the jungle. Why? Because he believed <u>he</u> was superior!

As I write these lines, I keep thinking of how blessed my life has been, how fortunate to have been born in the United States of America. I thank God, that Christ has paid for my sins, and for the men and women who, in combat, paid with their lives, the price of preserving my freedom.

Listen, I love my country, but it isn't perfect, never was, never will be. We can expect that; we remain in our fallen condition, imperfect, and in need of a savior. We mustn't forget that, but the point I want to make is, that much of the wealth America has produced, has been on the backs of the poor, there are additional consequences of the widespread acceptance of Darwinian science.

Slavery and the decimation of the Indians are ugly, permanent stains, on the pages of American history. By warfare, transmission of disease, and broken treaties, our Forefathers basically stole this country from the First Nation. And, it's true, among those who signed the *Declaration of Independence* there were slave holders. We are not called to judge those men. That remains the prerogative of Christ alone; but we can declare some of their policies as shameful and hypocritical. On the other hand, what they accomplished was by some standards, a miracle. It led many to believe it was God's providential hand that made it possible.

"(God) who rules by his might forever, whose eyes keep watch on the nations—let not the rebellious exalt themselves." (Psalm 66:7)

The Spread of Darwinism:
Unintended Consequences

The *State of Tennessee v. John Thomas Scopes, 1925*, commonly known as the *Scopes Monkey Trial*, was a farcical event staged to call attention to the community of Dayton, TN. A "comedy," I would call it, and I'll try to summarize it in as few words possible. The circumstances of the trial were beyond bizarre, but its outcome remains evident to this day.

In March 1925, Tennessee governor Austin Peay signed the *Butler Act*, making it unlawful for Tennessee educators to teach human evolution in the public schools. Such theories were considered nonsense by the community.

In April, the American Civil Liberties Union (ACLU) offered to defend any teacher accused of violating the *Butler Act*. Later, that month, a local business man recognized that the controversy over evolution was gaining momentum nationally. He met with the county superintendent of schools, and a local attorney, and convinced them that the highly emotional atmosphere of such a trial would bring the town of Dayton some much needed notoriety, boosting the local economy.

The attorney and school superintendent bought into the idea, and approached a teacher, John T. Scopes, with their plan to get the evolution issue before the court. Scopes agreed to "confess" that he had shared information with students in violation of the *Butler Act*. He even "coached" three of his students to testify that he had indeed discussed with them, the theory of human evolution. (Apes to Man)

On July 21, the well-publicized trial began. Reporters had poured in to Dayton to record the proceedings. Former presidential candidate, William Jennings Bryan, was representing the prosecution. Famed defense attorney, Clarence Darrow, would act in behalf of Mr. Scopes. Clearly, the nationally publicized trial was interpreted by the public, as a battle to determine whether the *Holy Bible* would continue to be the accepted source of Truth or, would that trust be given over to "modern" science, and educators. The prosecution's team supported the anti-evolution bill on religious grounds, describing evolution as "detrimental to our morality ... an assault on the very citadel of our Christian religion."

The trial itself was full of posturing back and forth by both sides. The presiding judge allowed the jury to hear a lot of testimony, only to have it expunged. Reports by H. L. Mencken, a popular author and journalist, described the 8-day proceedings as "unanimously hot for Genesis," and mocked the town's people as "yokels" and "morons." He called Bryan a "buffoon" and his speeches "theologic bilge." (en.wikipedia.org/wiki/Scopes_Trial)

In the end, Stokes was found guilty, fined $100.00, and released. So, the convoluted publicity stunt meant to bring recognition to Dayton, as a place where people could find opportunity, flopped; however, it did serve to stoke the fire that burned bridges between evolutionists and creationists regarding how science is taught in public schools.

There isn't a lot of agreement as to the cumulative effect of the Scopes trial, but in 1958, the *National Defense Education Act* was passed with the support of legislators fearing the United States education system was falling behind the Soviet Union. In a 1998 article, Randy Moore writes:

> "The act yielded textbooks, produced in cooperation with the *American Institute of Biological Sciences*, stressing the importance of evolution as the unifying principle of biology." (Moore, Randy, *The American Biology Teacher*, Vol. 60, No. 8 (Oct.1998), pp. 568-577)

(http://www.badnewsaboutchristianity.com/pics_05/1922moody.jpg)

Hatched in 1859, Darwinism is alive, but it is under attack. Scientists are armed with evidence produced by superpowered technology, showing without doubt, Darwin's theory of natural selection cannot stand. It is impossible for life to form spontaneously. It must have a predetermined templet of instructions.

The question becomes: Where and how do the instructions originate? Despite the Scopes trial, the controversy continues.

Given the number of religious and non-religious belief systems, that question begs controversy and disagreement. As a Christian, I believe in a living God, and in His wisdom and grace, has given humankind an invitation for everlasting life through Jesus, the Savior. God has also given us free-will, meaning that we can choose freely to accept, or reject that invitation.

Regardless of one's worldview, all require a leap of faith. I've made my choice. There is no riding the fence; either we believe in God, gods, or our own human capabilities. All must choose; not choosing is a choice.

In America, most people have at least some knowledge of the Gospel message. We have examined Darwin's worldview, and that of others who used Darwinism to justify their godless purposes. But what of the unbelievers, what do they believe?

John Dewey, an avowed humanist, whose beliefs about education and the superior capacity of socialism to govern fairly and equitably, provide a snapshot of the unbelievers' worldview, and some of the lies causing some to stumble.

The Spread of Darwinism:
Public Education and Socialism

Darwinism's power, to influence change that has profound long-term consequences, is clearly seen in the dramatic reform of public education by those who rely exclusively on the human intellect.

No one's worldview has affected the curricula of public schooling more than John Dewey (1859-1952) Father of Modern Education.

Perhaps you noticed Dewey's birthdate, 1859, the same year Darwin's book was published. In his adult life, Dewey was a professor at prestigious universities, including: Michigan, Chicago, and Columbia. He was heavily influenced by the writings of Darwin, and willingly accepted the theory of natural selection to be at the forefront of progressive (modern) thought. To quote his allegiance to Darwinism: "There is no God, and there is no soul. Hence, there are no needs for the props of traditional religion."

I interpret that to mean, that all teachings of Christ Jesus are props required by ignorant, primitive people, unfamiliar with modern thinking.

John Dewey was an unapologetic humanist and socialist, believing that one doesn't have to have God to be good, that groups of individuals can come together, united in a common cause, sharing principles and ideas to accomplish the desired outcome established by the group.

I would agree. The problem is, however, that in a larger society, getting that kind of agreement is highly unlikely. So, when the values and principles of the smaller groups begin to conflict, with the larger, whose over-arching standards shall determine a fair and just resolution? After all is said done, it seems we're left with but one question. Should the laws of men supersede those of God? Obviously, if there are only intelligent, modern, progressive thinkers, advocated by Dewey, then the matter is resolved.

Dewey also admired the success he believed he saw in Russia's approach to education. Couple that with Darwin's influence, add to it his affiliation with other progressive minds in academia, this is the result.

> **Human Manifesto I**
>
> The Manifesto is a product of many minds. It was designed to represent a developing point of view, not a new creed. The individuals whose signatures appear would, had they been writing individual statements, have stated the propositions in differing terms. The importance of the document is that more than thirty men have come to general agreement on matters of final concern and that these men are undoubtedly representative of a large number who are forging a new philosophy out of the materials of the modern world.

John Dewey's signature appears among those supporting the fifteen principles set forth in the American Humanists Association's theses, 1933.

Theses of Religious Humanism (Abridged)

Religious humanists believe and assert:

The universe is self-existing and not created.

Man is a part of nature and…has emerged as a result of a continuous process.

Man's religious culture and civilization…clearly depicted by anthropology and history, are the product of a gradual development (of) interaction with…natural environment and…social heritage…largely molded by…culture.

The nature of the universe depicted by modern science makes unacceptable any supernatural or cosmic guarantees of human values…the way to determine the existence and value of…all realities is by means of intelligent inquiry and…assessment of their relations to human needs.

Religion must formulate its…plans in the light of the scientific spirit and method…religion consists of those actions, purposes, and experiences which are humanly significant.

Nothing human is alien to the religious…labor, art, science, philosophy, love, friendship, recreation, all that is in…intelligently satisfying human living…distinction(s) between the sacred and the secular can no longer be maintained.

Religious Humanism considers the complete realization of human personality to be the end of man's life…its development and fulfillment in the here and now.

In place of old attitudes involved in worship and prayer, humanists' find…religious emotions expressed in a heightened sense of personal life and …cooperative effort to promote social well-being.

There will be no uniquely religious emotions and attitudes of the kind hitherto associated with belief in the supernatural.

Man will learn to face life in terms of his knowledge of their naturalness and probability… attitudes will be fostered by education, supported by custom…promote social and mental hygiene and discourage sentimental and unreal hopes and wishful thinking.

Religion must work increasingly for joy in living … foster the creative in man…encourage achievements …adding to the satisfactions of life…all associations exist for the fulfillment of life.

Intelligent evaluation, transformation, control, and direction of such associations and institutions with a view to enhancing human life, is the purpose of humanists.

Religious institutions, ritualistic forms, ecclesiastical methods, and communal activities must be reconstituted…rapidly…to function effectively in the modern world.

Existing acquisitive and profit-motivated society has shown itself to be inadequate…radical change in methods, controls, and motives must be instituted.

A socialized…cooperative economic order…established to…(assure) equitable distribution of the means of life…The goal of humanism is a free and universal society in which people voluntarily and intelligently cooperate for the common good.

Humanism will: affirm life rather than deny it; seek to elicit…possibilities of life, not flee from them, and endeavor to establish…conditions of a satisfactory life for all, not merely for the few.

(https://americanhumanist.org/what-is-humanism/manifesto1/)

These beliefs and Darwin's influence on John Dewey and other progressive-socialists remain, particularly in some of our colleges and universities, where freedom of speech and freedom of expression are being suppressed, while socialism is encouraged.

The Liar whispered, "Among men, you are wise, self-sufficient, not dependent on child-like fantasies to prop you up. Men will follow your lead and glorify your name. They will heap praise upon your name, and you will believe it is well deserved."

2

1953 - Hugh Hefner: *The Playboy Culture*

In December of 1953, I was a junior in high school, and was looking at the magazines displayed at Mr. Copeland's pharmacy at 25th St. and Farrington in Terre Haute, IN. Along with the comic books, *Sport, Sports Afield, Outdoor Life*—I noticed a magazine I hadn't seen before. I picked up a copy and began flipping through the pages when, whoa! What's this! I'm 16 years old, staring at a picture of Marilyn Monroe, fully airbrushed color, in her birthday suit! I thought to myself, this is a game changer!

Depending on your age, you might be laughing to think that was any big deal. Well, I can assure you that in the fifties, a large majority of teenagers were pretty naïve about sex, curious of course, but getting access to such matters was not easy. Nice people didn't talk about things of such intimate nature, at least not in mixed company.

Having sex outside of marriage was sinful, not that it didn't happen, and if it became public knowledge, even rumored, the guilty parties were shunned, and their reputations damaged. That's terrible, some of you are thinking. The hypocrisy is so clearly wrong.

I would agree, but we used to believe that two wrongs, didn't make a right.

The following month, *Playboy* wasn't on display with the other magazines. It could be purchased at the rear of the store, over the pharmacy counter. (Where it was rumored one could also purchase condoms!) I'm surprised that Mr. Copeland even continued to sell copies of *Playboy*.

In an online article, August 2017, Jennifer Rosenberg, wrote about that first edition. It was 44 pages, and no date on the cover because the 27-year-old Hefner wasn't sure there would be a second edition! He sold 54,175 copies, 50 cents a copy. The centerfold of MM wasn't posed for *Playboy*; it had been purchased from another source. (https://www.thoughtco.com/the-first-playboy-magazine-1779336)

Hefner's genius made him a multi-millionaire, but his influence on American culture goes way beyond his net worth. He recognized the energy of the male libido, and the desire for instant gratification in all things, but particularly sex. Let's be real; sex sells. As I mentioned earlier, in the fifties, sexual behavior was not openly discussed. *Playboy* was slick, suave, sophisticated, and with a wink, Hefner, by featuring articles appealing to men's intellect, was able to divert (some) attention away from the soft porn (Yeah, right.)

Playboy, in my opinion, because of the brand name and all it came to mean, was a game changer. In the greater scheme of things, war, poverty, corruption in high places, etc., airbrushed images of beautiful young women seem relatively innocent, harmless. Ah yes, close your eyes and you can hear the serpent's voice, so subtle and reassuring. Go ahead, you want it. You deserve it. Take it.

Appealing primarily to young men, but not excluding older men, Hefner's business acumen and marketing skill enabled him to establish an empire built on rebellion against traditional morals and family values. Sex, glamour, nudity, stylish materialism, and challenging authority, these were the templets for the monthly publication.

Elizabeth Fraterrigo, history professor, at Loyola University, Chicago, writes:

> "Its sexual content and glamorous depictions of bachelorhood made it roguish for the 1950s, but in its heyday, Playboy was more than a magazine filled with pictures of nude women and advice on how to make the perfect martini…It was, a crucial part of "mainstream debates about society, economics, and culture in postwar America."
> ("<u>Playboy and the Making of the Good Life in Modern America</u>" (Oxford University Press. 2009)

The initial shock of the attack on "Puritan" morals didn't last; freedom of speech prevailed (as it should), but as it always seems in America, when others began to imitate, they pushed it way beyond the limit. Sex, and in-your-face obscenities, photos leaving nothing to the imagination, with no thought of "sophisticated" lifestyles. These were magazines dedicated to exploiting the ugliest, rudest, crudest, perverted expressions of sexuality. It's the American way: Bigger, "badder," louder, more shocking, take it to the extreme! Thus, *Playboy* was an important factor leading to the sexual revolution of the sixties and seventies. American's worldview regarding sex was changed forever.

There are many, I'm sure, who defend Hef's agenda for achieving happiness and enjoying life less encumbered by "religion's oppressive morality" embracing modern ideas, intended to inspire young men of a generation ready to break from the chains of Puritanism.

As I stated earlier, I believe Hugh Hefner sold us soft porn, packaged along with well-written articles about art, music, philosophy, and literature. He surely considered himself to be the epitome of the Renaissance Man, educated, cultured, knowledgeable, and proficient in a wide range of subjects, but most importantly a liberated man.

There is a problem with being a liberated man as defined by Hefner's life style. By declaring ourselves free of any obligation to respect traditional roles, social, and economic expectations, we tend to set ourselves up as little gods, independent of lasting commitments outside ourselves. We don't live in a vacuum. Choices we make are like dropping a pebble in a pool, the ripples spread. To whom and how far, no one can say. Each pebble creates its own unique ripples. Hefner rejected spiritual values, finding beauty and pleasure in the material, substituting temporal truth for eternal Truth.

Certainly, he fulfilled his vision of happiness, but in his quest for liberation, he may have become entrapped in his own snare. What social values did Hefner promote that have taken hold of contemporary America? It is said he was financially supportive of causes aligned with his belief in women's rights for sexual freedom, civil rights, anything that lifted any control over individual choice. His advocacy for intercourse outside of marriage has undermined the sanctity of the monogamous relationship between one man and one woman.

The young women who willingly flocked to dress in the Bunny costume, or pose for a centerfold, weren't coerced. They listened to the serpent's voice. The money, the celebrity, an exciting lifestyle, you're entitled to it. What's the harm? So, now you wonder why women have been objectified? Hefner wasn't selling "sweethearts" to introduce to mother. He promoted "Playmates."

And, in a bit of irony, Hef may have unintentionally aligned himself with the Feminists and their legitimate push for equal rights and opportunities in the workplace. However, they also advocated the same freedom as men, to enjoy sex partners outside of marriage, and demanded the right to control their "own bodies." A not so subtle way of stating the pro-choice agenda that includes abortion on demand, a right affirmed by the Supreme Court of the United States. *(Roe v. Wade, 410 U.S. 113 (1973)* It was a controversial decision and remains so today.

Lest you think I'm being pious or self-righteous in pointing out the consequences of the *Playboy* brand, no; I'm guilty. I listened to the serpent's voice. My wife wasn't happy to see *Playboy* around the house or stashed in a closet hidden from the kids. Lying to myself, I rationalized, cutting myself some slack. Remember, earlier, I pointed out how easy it is to excuse our own flaws, when it serves our purpose.

"It's harmless," I'd say. "They're just airbrushed pictures. You know I love you." In a few years, the Internet, with a couple of clicks, allowed access to the raunchiest sites a human can devise. I couldn't deny the risk of going further. Too many professional colleagues were getting fired for having viewed inappropriate websites on their office computers.

A friend and I were discussing the increasing number of men wrestling with this issue. He said, "You know, it just kind of dawned on me, how disrespectful it is to my wife, to be looking at that stuff." He went on, "How would you feel if your wife was looking at pictures of other men? Even if she said they meant nothing, just pictures, would you really accept that as evidence of her complete, commitment to your marriage vows?"

I shared this anecdote with him. A senior member of the family had passed away, and the surviving adults were charged with cleaning closets, disposing of the useless, and separating out items to be kept. As we were removing boxes from closets, one of the women called, "Hey, come in here and look what I found." You guessed it, stacks of old "girlie" magazines.

It was an embarrassing, unfortunate situation. I told my friend, "At that point, I was determined that none of my family would discover a similar cache in my closet." Ashamed, I tossed the magazines and promised myself, and God, that I would recommit, recalling the sacred nature of my marriage vows.

"There is nothing covered up that will not be revealed and hidden that will not be known. Accordingly, whatever you have said in the dark shall be heard in the light, and what you have whispered in the inner rooms shall be proclaimed upon the housetops." (Luke 12:2-3)

How true it is! Anyone thinking their sins will not be revealed is a fool. Several years after having tossed the trash, the family was sitting around reminiscing about good ol' days of the kids' childhood. Our adult daughters teased me, "Yeah, Dad, we found the 'girlie' magazines in your closet." (The kids will search the house when you're not home.) We all laughed about it. But, it wasn't funny. It reminded me of the lie that had captured me, and how easily I accepted it. Hefner's legacy then, is—well, let him tell us.

"It's perfectly clear to me that religion is a myth. It's something we have invented to explain the inexplicable. My religion and the spiritual side of my life come from a sense of connection to the humankind and nature on this planet and in the universe."

"I am in overwhelming awe of it all: It is so fantastic, so complex, so beyond comprehension. What does it all mean—if it has any meaning at all? But how can it all exist if it doesn't have some kind of meaning?"

"I think anyone who suggests that they have the answer is motivated by the need to invent answers, because we have no such answers."

"The major civilizing force in the world is not religion, it's sex."

"We indeed did, and do, own our own minds and bodies, and anything from church or state that limits that is inappropriate and inconsistent with the society that America is supposed to be."

I leave it to you. Has Hefner's influence made America a better place to raise a family? It's not my intention to place the blame on Hefner. There's plenty of blame for all to share. The publishers of filth, and "music" that degrades women in the vilest ways, video games featuring sex and violence, suggestive TV ads, and programming that appeals to our basest instincts, all bear some blame.

A free pass can't be given to those who purchase filth, or to parents failing to provide adequate supervision and guidance for their children. The churches and their pastors choosing to ignore these issues, fearful someone in the congregation will be offended; all should be called out.

Pornography is real; it's widespread and pastors failing to confront the issue are guilty by their silence of perpetuating the lie that it's harmless.

Godless

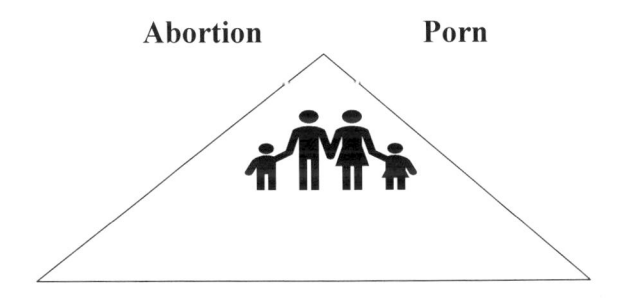

Abortion   **Porn**

Unrestrained Sexuality

1963 - Madalyn Murray O'Hair:

God Expelled from School

Many have likely never heard of Madalyn O'Hair, but in 1963, she became one of the most hated individuals in America. In this photo, she could be the stereotype of grandmother, not someone you might immediately associate with political activism and socialist reform. However, her aggressiveness as an atheist enabled her to change the way our nation's courts rule on cases having to do with the free expression of religious beliefs and the tradition of states' rights.

On February 27-28, 1963, the Supreme Court of the United States heard arguments on appeal from the Eastern District Federal Court of Pennsylvania, challenging the constitutionality of "sanctioned and organized Bible reading in public schools." The suit, in part, had been initiated by Madalyn Murray (O'Hair) against the Board of School Commissioners, Baltimore, MD. Her son, William, attended a public school in Baltimore. Daily policy and procedure included starting each day with a recitation of the *Lord's Prayer* and the reading of verses from the Bible.

Photo (https://cdn.quotesgram.com/small/59/9/883434944-MadalynMurrayOHair.jpg)

On June 17, 1963, Chief Justice Earl Warren handed down the 8-1 decision declaring that the above activities were unconstitutional. The ruling attested that reading scripture and reciting the *Lord's Prayer* are devotional, religious observances. Furthermore, the School Commissioners' claim that the observances were voluntary didn't match with the fact that school authorized personnel directed the daily activities as a matter of policy. It was also noted that readings required the use of the *Holy Bible*, indicating the school gave preference to the Christian faith. That decision clearly removed prayer from public schools, and the use of the Holy Bible, except as a tool in classic literature or comparative religions. O'Hair won the case.

Madalyn Murray O'Hair, the founder of the *American Atheists*, had become the poster girl for unbelievers. She was described as a brilliant, opinionated, flamboyant individual who could stir up a crowd. She actively sought to remove "In God We Trust" from U.S. currency, and to remove the phrase "under God" from the Pledge of Allegiance. O'Hair was unsuccessful in those attempts, but she continued to draw supporters for ideals she professed to be affiliated with Thomas Jefferson's views on the separation of church and state.

She was considered a difficult person to work for, basking in the attention of the press, while trashing her loyal employees. Because of her brazen personality and lack of appreciation for her supporters, she made enemies, including fellow atheists and secularists.

She was frequently harassed and received death threats. On August 27, 1995, O'Hair, her son, and granddaughter disappeared from her home in Austin, TX. David Roland Waters, a convicted murderer and former employee with the *American Atheists*, was a person of interest in the missing persons incident.

Following a protracted investigation, Waters, and another convicted felon were arrested, tried and convicted of the brutal slayings of the O'Hair family and a third felon, also murdered at the hands of Waters. In 2001, Waters told authorities about a site on a Texas ranch where they would eventually locate the dismembered remains of O'Hair and the other victims. Madalyn O'Hair, a soul tortured in life and in death, but her legacy of striving to rid society of all vestiges of God lives on.
(https://en.wikipedia.org/wiki/Madalyn_Murray_O'Hair)

To be fair, there is no outright intentional lie to be found in O'Hair's agenda. She believed in her cause. However, the lie that her life perpetuated is "there is no God;" therefore, in a modern society, intelligent people use science, not mythology, to inform their lives. We can trace her influence in some of the legal battles waged by unbelievers, in their ongoing attempts, to suppress completely, any public reference or behavior pertaining to God.

Her victory on behalf of unbelievers came on the shoulders of an earlier ruling by the Supreme Court in the case of *Engle v. Vitale, June 25, 1962*. Petitioners in New Hyde Park, New York, led by Steven Engle, complained that a voluntary prayer written by the State Board of Regents to "Almighty God" contradicted their religious beliefs. Led by Steven Engle, they challenged the constitutionality of the state's policy on school prayer.

The prayer reads: "Almighty God, we acknowledge our dependence upon Thee, and we beg Thy blessings upon us, our parents, our teachers and our country. Amen."

The majority opinion (6-1) delivered by Justice Hugo Black, ruled that government-written prayers were not to be recited in public schools in violation of the establishment clause of the *First Amendment*.

The Court explained that school prayer is a religious activity by its very nature, and that prescribing such a religious activity for school children violates the establishment clause. The program, created by government officials to promote a religious belief, was therefore unconstitutional.

The Court rejected arguments that people are not asked to join any specific established religion; and that the even though the prayer is voluntary, the Court held that the mere promotion of a religion is a violation, The Court further held that the fact that the prayer is worded generally, not to promote any particular religion is not a sufficient defense, because it promotes religions that recognize "Almighty God," which violates the Establishment Clause.

(I can't help it. Excuse me, Justice Black, but how in the world does mentioning Almighty God serve to establish a national religion?! Read it again! ***Congress shall make no law respecting an establishment of religion***." A government employee is in violation of federal law for participating in a prayer to Almighty God? What happened to the free exercise of religion? Did I miss a headline: *State Enacts Regents' Prayer into Law!*)

Having earned a law degree at South Texas College of Law, Houston, O'Hair was certainly aware of the *Everson v. Board of Education (1947)*, sixteen years prior to her suit against the Baltimore schools. Perhaps she took advantage of the lie originating in that case. In simple form, that I can understand, the story goes as follows.

A New Jersey law authorized local school boards to pay for transporting students to and from school, including private schools, most of which were Catholic. A local taxpayer Arch R. Everson, filed suit alleging that policy constituted aid to religion by reimbursing families for costs of attending religious schools; therefore, violating both the state and federal constitutions (*First Amendment*). Everson lost in the New Jersey Court of Errors and Appeals, then appealed to the U.S. Supreme Court. It agreed to hear the case.

On November 20, 1946, the case was argued before the court, Chief Justice Fred M. Vinson. On February 10, a 5-4 ruling was read favoring the Board's constitutional authority to reimburse families for transportation since payments were for all students and no tax dollars went to any religious institution. Clearly, families controlled the money.

Now the story takes a sharp turn. Both the major and dissenting opinions were broadly interpreted with respect to the *First Amendment's* establishment clause. It reads: "Congress shall make no law respecting an establishment of religion."

Let's begin with the dissenting opinion written by Justice Wiley Rutledge. He argued that the funds were raised by taxation, and their use did not give aid and encouragement to religious instruction; therefore, one can conclude that paying for transportation to school does not support religious instruction. (To me, that means not to any greater or lesser extent than reading, writing, and arithmetic. Thus, government's role remains neutral.)

Rutledge continued, noting that Thomas Jefferson and James Madison warned against "getting entangled in precedents." He wrote, "In this case, parents are reimbursed by money raised through taxation; it helps get their children to school, but it also aids them in a substantial way to get the very thing which they are sent to the particular school to secure, namely religious training and teaching."

In my mind, Rutledge makes the point that all families are helped equally when reimbursed by taxes raised for transporting students to the school of their choice. Is it any more, or less important to reimburse (or subsidize in part) transportation costs for families desiring that their student(s) attend a school having special emphasis on math & science, the arts, vocational training, or for special needs than it is for one seeking education with an emphasis on religion?

Justice Hugo Black presented the majority opinion. Let's take the time to examine his opinion in some detail. He begins. **"The 'establishment of religion' clause of the First Amendment means at least this: Neither a state nor the Federal Government can set up a church."** Take note. Justice Black is being loose with words here. Remember, the clause truly says, "Congress shall make no law…" Perhaps some would disagree with Black's statement Maybe the capital C in Congress is important? Could it mean to make a distinction between the federal government and state government?

The *Constitution* addresses the specifics of limited federal powers, leaving the remaining matters to the authority of the states. Our Forefathers clearly warned of the danger that the authority of the federal government would increase proportionate to its size, and by natural inclination begin usurping those powers originally given to the states. We are seeing that warning becoming the reality in America.

Black continues, **"Neither can (government) pass laws which aid one religion, aid all religions or prefer one religion over another."** Is it absolutely true that government, particularly a state, county, or municipality can't support "all religions" under any circumstance? Remember, the second clause of the *First Amendment* states that (Congress shall make no law) "prohibiting the free exercise thereof. (referring to religion)"

Black's language concerning the *First Amendment* is exceedingly broad in scope.

"Neither can (government) force nor influence a person to go to or to remain away from church against his will or force him to profess a belief or disbelief in any religion."

"No person can be punished for entertaining or professing religious beliefs or disbeliefs, for church attendance or non-attendance." Is this true? *Fox News, CBS,* and other media outlets covered an incident in October 2015, involving Joe Kennedy, a Bremerton WA, high school football coach. He was fired for kneeling at the fifty-yard line, following a game, engaging in a brief personal prayer. School officials cited concern that the district could be sued for violation of the *First Amendment*, believing that students and their parents witnessing a school employee praying on public school grounds would be interpreted as an endorsement of religion. Clearly an overreaction and misinterpretation of the freedom to freely express one's religious beliefs without punishment. Coach

Kennedy filed suit, claiming his religious rights had been violated. Is there doubt?

And, to add to the confusion, in 1969, when the *Tinker v. Des Moines* case was argued before the Supreme Court, I was an assistant principal in a metropolitan district high school, with an enrollment of nearly 4,000 students. It was a time of protest and civil disobedience. Schools were not spared.

In 1965, a high school student in Iowa, John Tinker and his sister Mary Beth Tinker, a junior high student, along with a few other students wanted to display their displeasure with our nation's policies related to the Vietnam war. Knowing the protest was in violation of district policy, they proceeded to tie black armbands around their sleeves and headed off to school. Upon arriving at their respective schools, they were quickly suspended, along with others for wearing apparel considered potentially disruptive.

The complaint was decided by the Supreme Court in February 1969. The ruling overturned the lower court's decision holding that the schools' first priority is to maintain a safe and orderly environment for instruction. We were shocked when Justice Abe Fortas wrote for the majority: "It can hardly be argued that either students or teachers shed their constitutional rights to freedom of speech or expression at the schoolhouse gate …"

It was a time of learning for all of us. But, the point I want to make in sharing that anecdote is that there's an obvious disconnect between the firing of Coach Kennedy and Justice Fortas' claim that "neither students or teachers shed their constitutional rights … at the schoolhouse gate." Would that also include religious speech and expression?

It's time to reexamine some of these decisions, rethinking the consequences of rulings by justices that have exceeded their authority.

Justice Black continues, **"No tax in any amount, large or small, can be levied to support any religious activities or institutions, whatever they may be called, or whatever form they may adopt to teach or practice religion.**

"Neither a state nor the Federal Government can, openly or secretly, participate in the affairs of any religious organizations or groups and vice versa."

Now, if I haven't lost you, keep in mind, the Court had just ruled that New Jersey was not in violation of any of the provisions noted above.

Justice Black closed the majority opinion stating: "In the words of Jefferson, the clause against establishment of religion by law was intended to erect 'a wall of separation between Church and State.'"

That Jefferson quote does not appear in the *Constitution*. The Supreme Court's singular responsibility is to interpret the Constitution and preserve its integrity as the basis for administering equal justice under the law for all, regardless of gender, race, religion, or social status.

You wouldn't think that the highest court of the land would use a phrase taken out of context, from a note written in January 1802, by Thomas Jefferson, to the Danbury Connecticut Baptists Association, thanking them for acknowledging his support of religious liberty, as the court's sole basis for stifling, repressing, religious freedom.

But, that is what has happened. Read the main part of the note for yourself.

> "Believing with you that religion is a matter solely between Man & his God, that he owes account to none other for his faith or worship, that the legitimate powers of government reach actions only, & not opinions,
>
> "I contemplate with sovereign reverence that act of the whole American people declaring that their legislature should 'make no law respecting an establishment of religion, or prohibiting the free exercise thereof,' thus building a wall of separation between Church & State.
>
> "Adhering to this expression of the supreme will of the nation in behalf of the rights of conscience, I shall see with satisfaction the progress of those sentiments restoring to man his natural rights, convinced he has no natural right in opposition to his social duties." Thomas Jefferson, Jan. 1, 1802.
> (The Library of Congress > Information Bulletin > June 1998)

No one can say with certainty what Jefferson expressly meant. Justice Hugo Black determined it meant, "an impregnable wall from which we dare not remove a single stone."

How can an obscure document that had nothing to do with the *Constitution*, become the instrument that legislates against religious liberty as defined in the First Amendment? There's nothing new in this; people have forever complained about personal bias overshadowing the objectivity of those who wear the black robes. Truth is, it's time to revisit the context of Black's "impregnable wall of separation" and evaluate the political bias that supports it.

Before wrapping up the saga of Madalyn Murray O'Hair and the role of an overly zealous Supreme Court in suppressing the relationship between government and religion, let's take a last look at the belief of Thomas Jefferson.

"No nation has ever yet existed or been governed without religion— nor can be. The Christian religion is the best religion that has been given to man and I, as Chief Magistrate of this nation, am bound to give it the sanction of my example."

ThomasJefferson/Bearlakerendezvous.com

Jefferson' writings document his strong belief in the integrity of the individual states to govern closer to home, avoiding the danger of too much power vested at the federal level and its inherent inclination toward growth and control. Given that fact, coupled with his support of legislation to support religion (Example: allocating federal dollars to build schools and educate Indian children with emphasis on religious values.) would make it hard to believe that he would agree with the stifling attitude toward religion that is law of the land today.

It's been more than a half-century since Madalyn Murray O'Hair claimed her "15 minutes" of fame. As I've read her story, I find it sad. When all is said and done, we're so much more alike than different. Gender, pigmentation, age, about any way you want to cut it, there are a few basic things all humans need. One of them is love—to love and be loved. She never found the love that she craved. As Johnny Lee's 1980 hit country tune said, she was "lookin' for love in all the wrong places."

> *"I am good,*
>
> *I am not an angel.*
>
> *I do sin,*
>
> *but I am not the devil.*
>
> *I am just a small girl,*
>
> *in a big world trying to find*
>
> *someone to love."*.
>
> Marilyn Monroe
>
> (1926-1962)

For a variety of reasons, including broken relationships, it appeared O'Hair became embittered and succumbed to the serpent's lie. God is holding out on you. Just take what you want; you're smart, smarter than most. You're better than they are. Don't trust anyone; depend only yourself. You're entitled to have anything you want. You don't need God.

Madalyn O'Hair's mission as an atheist never fully materialized, but what she was able to accomplish gave the unbelievers hope. They were emboldened, gaining strength as a legitimate political force, and using the courts to call attention to a godless agenda, demanding the complete separation of Church and State, to the end that religion is an enemy of the State.

A recent survey by the Pew Forum on Religion and Public Life found that slightly more than 16 percent of Americans are unbelievers. In the Pew survey, on the question of religion, 51 million Americans checked "None," raising the percent of unbelievers to more than one in five. (Agnostics, atheists, humanists) As a group, they're better organized now; give credit to O'Hair for her influence.

David Niose, Legal Director, of the Appignani Humanist Legal Center, Washington, D. C., is among the strongest voices in America legislating for freedom from religion. Having served as president of the American Humanist Association and the Secular Coalition for America, Niose, is a prolific writer; those interested in learning why unbelievers are aggrieved by religion, can keep up with their legal activities at *davidniose.com*. The latent coach in me believes it's a good practice to remain in touch with the opposition's thinking.

4

1971: The Pentagon Papers:
Lies Revealed

It would be naïve of us to believe that leaders always tell the truth, but as citizens, we would like to believe that our rulers, although they may be excused for withholding certain information from us in matters of national security, but outright lying, intentionally lying to us? No, we'd rather not believe that. But, over the past half-century there have been so many confirmed instances of people in high places, including presidents and priests, standing before the American people and the world, knowingly lying to us. Once it may have been shocking; now it's barely newsworthy.

The Pentagon Papers, commissioned in 1967 by Secretary of Defense, Robert McNamara, is an official historical account of America's policies and objectives related to the Vietnam war. The stunning lies of federal officials revealed in that report have had a lasting effect on our country and contributed greatly to the divisiveness and disillusionment that confounds us yet today.

The Post, a 20th Century-Fox film produced and directed by Steven Spielberg released in December of 2017, begins with events of the early seventies setting the stage for describing how and why the classified documents contained in *The Pentagon Papers* were leaked to the public, shocking the nation, shaking to the core, its trust in those we elect to represent us.

Our troubles in Vietnam began following WWII with our good intention of containing the spread of communism in Southeast Asia. The Administrations of Presidents Truman and Eisenhower both failed to grasp the nature of the culture and politics that led to the bloody struggle sucking the United States into a protracted conflict lasting from 1946 until 1976. It's doubtful that either lied to the public; however, as perfect Monday morning quarterbacks, we can accuse them of calling the wrong plays.

One of the many authors contributing to the content of *The Pentagon Papers* was Daniel Ellsberg, a young reporter and military analyst, who had spent two years as a volunteer with Marines in combat. He noted serious discrepancies between what he had observed, what was being reported to the folks back home, and the content of official classified reports. Becoming disillusioned with the conduct of the war, Ellsberg decided to share his knowledge with lawmakers, hoping the discrepancies between fact and fancy would be investigated. No takers—he knew those leaking classified information could be charged with treason.

Frustrated and angry that officials at the highest levels of our government, were intentionally, systematically, deceiving the nation about the motives and progress of the war, Ellsberg turned his attention to newspaper publishers. With the help of a few trusted colleagues, he began removing classified documents from secured files and copying them a few at a time until the entire report had been photocopied. He and his colleagues distributed copies to newsrooms across the country, hoping one would make the lies and deceit public.

The *New York Times* scooped the other papers, publishing the first installment on June 13, 1971; reporter, Neil Sheehan, introduced America to the truth.

Presidents Kennedy, Johnson, and Nixon were guilty of misleading (lying to) the media and the public about the role of the United States in Vietnam. Kennedy hid the fact that in 1961 he approved escalating our support for South Vietnam by sending them helicopters and Green Beret troop advisors. He confided in a colleague he did not want to be the president that lost a war. He was assassinated by a sniper's bullet in November 1963, while riding in a motorcade in Dallas. As successor, Lyndon B. Johnson was sworn in as our 36th president.

The timing for LBJ, as he was known, couldn't have been less fortunate. The charismatic Kennedy and his family were beloved by the public, national mourning of his death was genuine. Meanwhile, conditions in Vietnam continued to worsen.

In August 1964, following an alleged communist attack on two U.S. destroyers positioned off the coast of Vietnam, Congress signed the *Gulf of Tonkin Resolution* authorizing Johnson to take all necessary measures against any further aggression by North Vietnam. It wasn't a declaration of war, but the effect was the same. LBJ became the fourth president to be Commander-in-Chief of a war recognized to be unwinnable. The bombing increased, the scope of conflict stretched into neighboring countries Laos and Cambodia. The body count accelerated.

In homes across America, on college campuses, on Wall Street, in the hearts and minds of individuals everywhere, the revelations in *The Pentagon Papers* had divided the country into factions, opposite ends of a continuum. Young men burned draft cards; others went across the border into Canada to avoid conscription. Daniel Ellsberg was widely condemned as a traitor. Disturbing TV images from Southeast Asia began to undermine the public's confidence in Johnson and his administration. Angry protests from both sides broke out. His lies and those of his predecessors began to catch up with him. LBJ was, without doubt under terrible stress.

Johnson, Attorney General John Mitchell, and others within the government, tried to halt the publication of *The Pentagon Papers*. (Knowing that the report would convict them and damage the credibility of future administrations. Should we be surprised?) They pursued the claim that publishers had no authority to divulge classified documents. A New York Federal Court immediately slapped *The Times* with a temporary restraining order and warned *The Washington Post* of the same. With the *Times* sidelined, Ben Bradlee, editor of *The Post,* ignored the court's threat. The news continued to shed light on the lies and deceit of those in high places. On June 30, 1971, the case was heard by The Supreme Court. Its ruling favored the nation's newspapers—freedom of the press!

I like to think of LBJ as a decent man, caught up in circumstances beyond his capacity to control. A flawed man at the end of his rope, wanting to preserve his sense of integrity, deceiving himself to justify the continuation of a lost cause, sending young people into that horrific war, yet knowing it was wrong. He couldn't find the courage to stand before the American public and admit—We have lost.

I offer no condemnation. He was under tremendous pressure from all sides. He surely felt the anger and frustration of a nation fed up with a political conflict in which we had little at stake, had lasted some thirty years, and at a cost of two trillion dollars by today's value. LBJ left office in January 1969, retired to his ranch in Texas, and in 1973, died of a heart attack at age 64. I honestly believe he was a casualty of the war. Stress kills. He likely was blessed not to have lived to witness the fall of Saigon!

Secretary of Defense, Robert McNamara, and General William Westmoreland, Commander of U. S Forces in Vietnam, 1964-1968, were both guilty of lying about the purpose and the progress of the Vietnam war. McNamara recognized early on that our policies were misguided, politically and militarily—he failed the families of those whose sons and daughters continued in combat, risking death in a war he knew, "was unwinnable."

"Pride goeth before destruction, and a haughty spirit before a fall." (Proverbs 16:18)

Westmoreland repeatedly inflated the enemy body count. His ego wouldn't allow him to acknowledge his combat strategies weren't working. Even though he was reporting that our soldiers were winning by a body bag ratio of 10-1, our forces were not able to show progress. He deceived himself, Congress, and the public. Neither Westmoreland or McNamara suffered any formal rebuke. (https://en.wikipedia.org/wiki/Pentagon_Papers)

In January 1969, Richard M. Nixon became the fifth president to confront North Vietnam. He intended to continue to escalate the war with increased bombing runs and force negotiations for a peaceful settlement bringing an end to the war. Secretary of State Henry Kissinger tried unsuccessfully to get the North Vietnamese leaders to make concessions. (Probably because they knew they didn't have to; they were in control.) For the next four years that strategy continued with little success.

On the home front, Nixon was holding his own. Troop withdrawals were a salve for the emotional wounds of an America tired of three decades of lies, excuses, and ineffective military strategy. However, on Aug. 8, 1974, President Ricard M. Nixon, resigned from office after it was learned that he lied about his involvement in an attempted break-in at the Democratic National Committee headquarters in the Watergate complex, Washington, D.C.

So now the sword had passed to President Gerald Ford, who took the oath of office in August 1974. He continued the troop withdrawals and let up on the bombing. It was apparent the South Vietnamese would soon be responsible for their destiny.

In an address on the campus of Tulane University, New Orleans, April 23, 1975, President Gerald Ford, humbled himself before the nation, and declared "The war in Vietnam is finished as far as the United States is concerned."

On April 30, 1975, following days of massive helicopter evacuations of U.S. troops, civilian personnel, and Vietnamese refugees, tanks of The Peoples' Army of North Vietnam rolled into the South Vietnam capital of Saigon.

"How the mighty have fallen! The weapons of war have perished!" (2 Samuel 1: 25-27)

Ten years later President Ford, in an interview with Bob Woodward and Christine Parthemore of *The*

Washington Post, was asked how he dealt with the mess he was handed. President Ford said this:

> "We inherited the problem with the job...my obligation on behalf of the country is to try and solve the damn thing. You know, there was a fundamental mistake made after WW II, when the French had committed to support the Vietnamese...I went down to Saigon [in 1953] ... to find out why we're going to spend a lot of money...on behalf of the South Vietnamese...all these French generals and colonels...telling me how they were gonna win the war against the [North] Vietnamese.
>
> "Well, it sounded good on paper, and they ought to know more than I did. Well, in about six months the French got the hell kicked out of them in Dien Bien Phu ... The point is, we were on the wrong side of the locals. We made the same mistake that the French did, except we got deeper and deeper in the war. We could have avoided the whole darn Vietnam War if somebody in the Department of Defense or State had said, "Look here. Do we want to inherit the French mess?"
> (http://www.washingtonpost.com/wpdyn/content/article/2006/12/29/AR2006122901240.html)

> *"But you have planted wickedness, you have reaped evil, you have eaten the fruit of deception. Because you have depended on your own strength and on your many warriors, the roar of battle will rise against your people."* (Hosea 10: 13-14)

The Wall, the Vietnam War Memorial, Washington, D.C., was dedicated in 1982. As of May 20, 2017, there are

58,318 names etched into 144 panels. Each name has a story, family and friends, who remember them when.

Unfortunately, presidents caught up in their own lies continued after Vietnam. President William J. Clinton (1993-2001), lied about his relationship with a female aide and other women who brought forward charges of sexual misconduct. He was acquitted of all charges. The congressional voting went along party lines. Democrats held the majority.

In 2003, President George W. Bush was accused of lying about an alleged buildup of "weapons of mass destruction" being hidden by Iraqi president, Saddam Hussein. Many leaders at home and abroad believed Hussein indeed had a stockpile of weapons because they had been used against his own people. An international team of inspectors scoured Iraq. No weapons were uncovered. Despite what some believe to the contrary, there has been no proof that the president lied. But, the lies of previous presidents had sown the seeds of doubt.

In the 2007-2008, presidential campaign, Barack Obama, told America the *Affordable Care Act* would be "making health insurance universal." (that means 100 percent) Not true. We'll chalk that one up as a "campaign promise." However, there can be no doubt that as president, his oft-repeated promise, "If you like your health care plan, you can keep it," was intentional, a lie promoting his signature piece of legislation. That lie cost him dearly in terms of his credibility; otherwise, he was not held accountable for intentionally misleading those he had sworn to serve and protect.

Under the administration of Donald Trump, our nation has been severed and shredded by raw emotion.

Reactions to President Trump's tweets range from blind unswerving support on the extreme right to blind, unyielding, unapologetic hatred on the extreme left. Each of the three branches of our government have become suspicious, disrespectful, accusatory factions that have lost their way, seemingly incapable of legislating in behalf of those who elected them.

"These people are grumblers and faultfinders; they follow their own evil desires; they boast about themselves and flatter others for their own advantage." (Jude 16).

Whose truth can we believe? Political posturing, economic policies, gun legislation, immigration reform, tax reform—none of it will make America great again. Only a people willing to repent, humble themselves before their Creator, and returning to the spiritual values upon which the nation was founded—only then will hearts be changed. A godless nation will never achieve greatness. That is a Truth you can believe.

Nothing is more dangerous than sincere ignorance and conscientious stupidity.

Dr. Martin Luther King, Jr.(http://unitedway-cny.org/mlk-foodclothing-drive/mlking)

5

Roe v. Wade:

Abortion on Demand

It was spring, 1981, a doctor sat facing a Senate Subcommittee of the Ninety-Seventh Congress of the United States. He had been called to give testimony related to *The Human Life* bill, S.158. The question before him was: When does human life begin? He said, "From a biological perspective the question of when life begins cannot be disputed by philosophers or theologians; it is a scientific fact, life begins at the moment of conception. When the female egg is fertilized by the male sperm, a new life is created, unique, unlike any other past or in the future. In my reading and research, I don't believe anyone has disproved this fact."

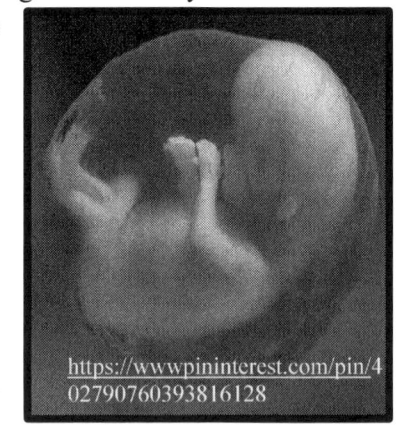

https://www.wpininterest.com/pin/402790760393816128

Following his testimony another highly regarded doctor took his turn addressing the same question. He answered, "Truthfully, no one can say exactly when one becomes a 'human' being complete with consciousness of one's self. It is not mere biological presence in the species, *homo sapiens*, that makes one a human being. Only at the point that the living being can consciously control and

110

manage its life has it achieved its humanity, otherwise, it remains an animal. Shocking, is it not, to consider that an infant is not a human being?" He concluded by saying, "It is not biology that determines the intrinsic worth and value of a human life." (http://www.epm.org/resources/2011/Apr/27/when-does-life-begin-quotes-many-sources/SarahTerzo)

Two distinguished doctors, each testifying, responding to the same question, each expressing his opinion conscientiously, based on extensive training and experience. They seem at opposite ends of a continuum and we should not be surprised. One answered with an emphasis on science. The other answered with an emphasis on a moral and ethical point of view. When addressing the practice of abortion, and when attempting to define what it means to be "human," both are essential considerations.

At the point of conception, life begins; there is no argument to be made otherwise. However, we are divided on the question of what it means to be human. Biologically, then, that means if left to continue its unique genetic development, a fetus will mature through its predetermined templet and become a person. It will never be just an "animal!" The sperm and egg will produce a human being, not a dog or a cat. There can be no argument on that point.

The argument, then, is a moral and ethical one. What is the value, the worth, of a human? How much are you worth? Why? If you're married, how much is your spouse worth? How much do you value your children? What about the lives of those who, for whatever reasons, are born with a physical defect—worth less or more? Whose life is more important? King or slave? Rich or poor? Male or female? Mother or child? The Supreme Court was not adequately prepared to address these questions at the time it issued the ruling deciding *Roe v. Wade (1973)*.

It was in deliberating that case that caused the Supreme Court to declare, "When those trained in the respective disciplines of medicine, philosophy, and theology are unable to arrive at any consensus, the judiciary, at this point in the development of man's knowledge, is not in a position to speculate as to the answer."

The Court went on to explain that with respect to the "sensitive and difficult" question of when life begins, the lack of agreement in this matter left the Court unable to resolve the question: When does life begin? Although it acknowledged its limitations, the Court went ahead with the case and ultimately ruled in favor of abortion on demand. That is where we stand today.

The Liar whispered, "There is no god; just look around you at the worldwide death and destruction; generation following generation, babies and children, mothers and fathers, displaced by wars and famine. How can you say there is a god that created them and then allows them to suffer all manner of starvation, disease, and persecution? No, now is your time, seize it. That bump in your tummy will hold you back, tie you down, just get rid of it and get on with pursuing your dreams."

The doctor at the clinic told her it was a simple procedure. Removing the mass would be completely safe, and "no one needs to know." The Holy Spirit spoke to her. "You have eaten of the fruit; therefore, you know the difference between good and evil. You understand the 'mass' is a child, your child." Crunch time! I didn't want this to happen, she told herself. I'm not a criminal. I just want things to be back to normal. This is my legal right—but is it right? How can I ever make this choice? She cried.

A teenage girl wrote in her diary, "I don't know your name, or who you are, or where you are. I don't know why you gave me away, but I'm so grateful you gave me life. I have many blessings for which I'm thankful. I pray that all things worked out for you and that you are happy. Today is my thirteenth birthday. I wonder if you wished me a happy birthday?"

These emotionally charged anecdotes serve as a reminder that all of us are confronted, at times, by life's circumstances forcing a choice between that which we inherently understand is right or wrong. We all recognize that under laws created by man, there is wiggle room; "just because it's legal, doesn't make it right." There's the opportunity to go ahead with a choice we clearly know is immoral, unethical, or unjust, but the law gives permission. Go ahead, sell electronic games that glorify violence and gunning people down—it's legal. What's the harm?

When we rely on man's laws, it's easy to think we can outsmart the law—ignore it. Who will know? When we abide in the eternal laws of the Living God, there is no wiggle room. God's laws are immutable, carved in stone. We understand whether other people ever know of our evil deeds or not, and we're not held accountable in this life, our secrets will not be hidden from God and we'll answer for them in the presence of The Creator.

On January 22, 1973, the Supreme Court of the United States issued its 7-2 decision favoring the plaintiff, Roe, overturning an earlier interpretation of abortion rights by a Texas court. Some felt it was a great victory for women's rights, a legal declaration granting them control over decisions affecting their personal health and well-being. Others were dismayed that the decision denied the right to life, a human life unable to testify on its own behalf. The *US Abortion Clock.org* count stands at more than 60 million lives snuffed since *Roe v. Wade*. Controversy over abortion sorely divides America.

One of the key arguments in the case revolved around the question: When does life begin? Remember, in 1973, the Supreme Court didn't have the testimonies of the medical and scientific communities establishing the indisputable fact that life begins at conception. There were four options. Some believed life begins the moment the sperm fertilizes the egg. (As was established by the 1981 Senate Subcommittee hearings on S.158, *The Human Life* bill.) Some believed human life begins within the period of 24-28 weeks when the child is fully formed. Some believed life begins when the child leaves the womb. Before we look at the fourth option, let's take a quick look at how God's Truth has been twisted when mankind substitutes its values in place of the Creator's.

For example, the concept of life remains contorted by extreme pro-life double-talk, attempting to justify cases of full-term abortion, some pro-life folks call it cold-blooded murder. How many are performed each year is hard to nail down. Obviously, unlawful cases aren't reported; however, in 2014 the Center for Disease Control and Protection reported 1.3 percent of the more than 652,000 were performed in the third trimester. Not a large number, you might say, but it was one-hundred percent for those that were aborted. And, before we dismiss the number as insignificant, we should understand how these lives end.

"D&X" (dilation and extraction) The woman's cervix is dilated. If necessary, the fetus is rotated until it is facing feet downwards. The surgeon reaches into the uterus

and pulls the fetus' body, (except for) its head, out of the woman's body. Surgical scissors are inserted into the base of the fetal skull and withdrawn. A suction tube is inserted, and the fetus' brains are removed through aspiration. This partially collapses the fetal skull. The fetus is then fully removed from the woman's body.
(http://legaldictionary.thefreedictionary.com/partial-birth+abortion)

If that "fetus" (a medical term meaning "offspring") is alive prior to the procedure, is that not murder? Some, who favor pro-choice, believe a fetus is akin to a premature baby, not capable of surviving outside the womb; therefore, not a viable life form. A fetus, early in the third trimester (24-28 weeks) is medically defined as viable, i.e., capable of living with support outside the womb.

Given that definition, it seems outrageous for those going so far as to say, a fetus is not a baby until the mother gives it birth. That kind of thinking flies in the face of what scientists and physicians have agreed on. However, we are still left with the issue raised earlier. Can an infant be considered a "human" before it acquires consciousness of its self? Is it mere biological presence in the species, *homo sapiens*, that makes one human? Is it at the point when a living being can consciously control and manage its life that it has achieved its humanity? Is it more than biology that determines the intrinsic worth and value of a human life?

When Does Life Begin? Sarah Terzo provides an indisputable answer in an online article appearing in *Eternal Perspective Ministries.*
(https://www.epm.org/resources/2010/Mar/2/quotes-abortion-clinic-workers-and-doctors-former-/)

My conclusion is science says life begins at the point of conception. We are lying to ourselves if we say otherwise. That fourth option I mentioned earlier, is an affirmation that life is sacred.

"For you formed my inward parts; you knitted me together in my mother's womb. I praise you, for I am fearfully and wonderfully made. Wonderful are your works; my soul knows it very well. My frame was not hidden from you, when I was being made in secret, intricately woven in the depths of the earth. Your eyes saw my unformed substance; in your book were written, every one of them, the days that were formed for me, when as yet there was none of them."(Psalm 139:13-16)

These verses remind us that in the first trimester the fetus isn't just a blob, not yet human. We can safely say, the DNA instructions in that "blob" are uniquely encoded to produce a human being, and what's more, that DNA is for one of a kind. Just like you. Miraculous, is it not?

Some try to make the evolution argument credible by noting that there is approximately a two-percent difference in the DNA of humans and chimpanzees, implying a common ancestry. Creationists and evolutionists alike expect to find similarities and differences, but until the evolutionists can explain the significance of the two-percent difference between the genetic chemistry of chimps and humans, I'll side with faith in Genesis 1: 26-28, God created man to have dominion over everything that is upon the earth. In other words, there is man—and then—there is everything else!

Look, I'm not a scientist or physician. I'm a man talking about an emotionally charged issue that divides the nation to the point that disagreement, on either side of the question, is tantamount to the worst kind of evil. Protesters march, slogans are shouted, speeches are made, too often resorting to profanity, name-calling, blaming, and shaming the opposition, and calling it, "standing up" for the rights of women. When that kind of tone is set, civil debate is even more difficult.

Gallup polls, 1975-2017, consistently reveal, that with respect to questions related to when, or if, abortion should be lawful, roughly between 50-56 percent of the adults surveyed believe there are special circumstances when aborting a child can be morally and medically justified. Nearly 30 percent believe that it should be legal in all circumstances, and those who say never, make up roughly 12 -18 percent of those surveyed.
(https://news.gallup.com/poll/211901/abortion-attitudes-stable-no-consensus-legality.aspx)

These data suggest to me that perhaps America is not as divided as the protesters make it seem. Shrill voices shouting obscenities, and outrageous speeches that include thoughts of "blowing up the White House," or calling abortion "cold-blooded murder," such extreme language does little to provide the kind of support any woman needs when confronted with this life, or death decision.

All, whether favoring pro-choice or pro-life, should respect the rights of both the mother and the child (and the father). Lives are at stake, families disrupted, and decisions second-guessed. Let's find it in our hearts to judge less, forgive more, and acknowledge the fact, that in the end such intimate choices are not ours to make for others.

It's my guess our nation will remain divided over this matter, but the militant, confrontational attitudes must be overcome, replaced by a renewed sense of reverence for the sanctity of life. It troubled me that since 1975, the recent poll showed nearly a 10% increase in the number of adults who believe abortion should be lawful under any circumstances. If that is a trend, it's in the wrong direction.

Who will speak on behalf of the unborn? Do you not think God will hold us accountable?

In a 1989 *New York Times* article, a voice was heard in behalf of the lives that have been aborted—Norma McCorvey, "More and more," she said, "I'm the issue. I don't know if I should be the issue. Abortion is the issue. I never even had an abortion." (Napikoski, Linda. "Norma McCorvey." ThoughtCo, Jun. 14, 2018, thoughtco.com/norma-mccorvey-abortion-3528239)

McCorvey had placed her child up for adoption because she said, "We live in a society today where these children can be wanted children. Even if you don't want to keep this child after you've had it, there's plenty of young couples out there, that want children."
(https://www.brainyquote.com/authors/norma_mccorvey)

She also stated, "I think it's safe to say that the entire abortion industry is based on a lie. I am dedicated to spending the rest of my life undoing the law that bears my name." *(https://www.brainyquote.com/authors/norma_mccorvey)*

Perhaps you know, if not, you should know that Norma Leah McCorvey is best known as the plaintiff Jane Roe, *Roe v. Wade (1973)*. She tells her inspiring story in *Won by Love* and *I Am Roe*.

(Check thriftbooks.com and amazonbooks.com for editions.) Norma Leah McCorvey 1947-2017(Photo:: en.wilkipedia.org)

6

Sphere Sovereignty: *Trashing Individual Rights*

Before we discuss this lie that divides us, we need to understand the concept of sphere sovereignty, a term unfamiliar to many of us. What does it mean and why is it important?

Abraham Kuyper (1837-1920), a theologian, journalist, and founder of the *Reformed Churches in the Netherlands*, was Prime Minister of the Netherlands between 1901 and 1905. His philosophy of the relationship between society and government was primarily motivated by his Christian religious orientation, that is the creation, fall, and redemption of man through the life, death, and resurrection of Christ. It was in attempting to find the proper balance among the rights of individual citizen, the role of religion, and the power of government, that led him to develop the concept of sphere sovereignty. *(en.wikipedia.org/wiki/Sphere-sovereignty)*

Fast forward: On 18 April 2008, a paper was presented at the *Abraham Kuyper Center* at *Princeton Theological Seminary*; the author of the paper was Herman Dooyeweerd, (1894-1977) a Dutch juridical scholar and philosopher. Gregory Baus, (M.A., philosophy, University of Amsterdam, 2006) was presenting Dooyeweerd's response to Kuyper's concept. It was generally accepted that Kuyper had adequately explained the qualities of sovereignty but had failed to specifically identify which areas of human society could claim the status of sovereignty. Dooyeweerd outlined a taxonomy of fifteen natural spheres that would include family and marriage, to be distinguished from organized spheres such as church and government. He clearly emphasized the gut level emotions involved in attempting to align the opposing worldviews of believers and unbelievers. No condemnation is allowed, no pointing fingers, or shaking fists at the other side.

"Live as free people...show respect for all men (treat them honorably). Love the brotherhood, the Christian fraternity of which Christ is the head." (1 Peter 16-17)

Like Kuyper, Dooyeweerd was coming from a Christian point of view; God is the creator of all things and all things respond to His sense of order and priorities, therefore, He governs all things.

"And God said, "Let the land produce living creatures according to their kinds: the livestock, the creatures that move along the ground, and the wild animals, each according to its kind." And it was so." (Genesis 1:24)

This says to me that each of God's creations has a kind of internal integrity that separates one from the other, yet all interact in harmony with the overall design of creation. Each kind is sufficient unto itself and will thrive unless its integrity is compromised by another kind. These spheres are essential to a nation that guarantees its citizens freedom to pursue life, liberty, and the pursuit of happiness.

120

Unencumbered by the heavy hand of government, the sheep will do just fine until the wolf arrives.

In his paper, Dooyeweerd emphasized the absolute sovereignty of God, meaning that as human societies form, each has an intrinsic nature with specific corresponding laws of life. These fundamental laws are not derived from the authority of any other sphere, but by God alone. (Think marriage.) Dooyeweerd's work establishes the distinct qualities that define the various spheres and their unique roles necessary to the survival of societal communities.

Such spheres are autonomous having wholeness within themselves, none valued more than the others—no hierarchical position. This is an important concept reflected in our *Constitution*! Three co-equal branches of government, each performing a distinct role, independent of the other two, but accountable for staying within the boundaries of its unique function, not interfering in the workings of the other.

At this point, we don't need to examine Dooyeweerd's work in its depth because it is considerable. If you're interested in pursuing it further, you can find it at www.*Kuyper and Dooyeweerd: Sphere Sovereignty and Modal Aspects/Tim Keene.*

To expose the lie, let's look at five societal spheres that could be considered autonomous, that is, given by God, not derived from the authority of any other sphere. As we go, we'll discover the consequences to each sphere when its integrity is co-opted by another sphere.

1. The Sovereignty of The State: From this point on, I'll be using the words government and State interchangeably, The State being that civil authority of local, state, or federal government, the sphere that carries the sword of justice by which righteousness is protected and evil is curtailed, by force if necessary.

Earlier, I referred to *The Truth Project*, produced by Focus on the Family. In the ninth segment of that DVD series, the sphere of government is examined. Some readers will likely point out that the *Holy Bible* doesn't specify the ideal form of government or details for governing. They would be correct on that point, but it has words enough regarding what is required of rulers and citizens, that we can knit together God's clear command to those chosen to rule over the affairs of The State.

"But Jesus called them to him and said, "You know that the rulers of the Gentiles lord it over them, and those who are great exercise authority over them. It shall not be so among you. But whoever would be great among you must be your servant, and whoever would be first among you must be your slave, even as the Son of Man came not to be served but to serve, and to give his life as a ransom for many." (Matthew 20: 25-28)

It doesn't get much clearer than that. In the words of the apostle Peter, *"Shepherd the flock of God which is among you, serving as overseers, not by compulsion but willingly, not for dishonest gain but eagerly; nor as being lords over those entrusted to you, but being examples to the flock."* (1 Peter 5:2-3)

We can believe that God calls those who represent the authority of The State to serve willingly, protecting the interests of the people, not for selfish gain, but with humility as trusted examples of good citizenship. (Humility meaning without arrogance, pride, or sense of entitlement.)

The State serves as an excellent example of an organized sphere of society as opposed to a natural sphere—marriage. It doesn't derive its authority from any other sphere; it has been given by God alone to serve His purpose—condone good, punish evil, encourage morality and ethics, uphold the law, defend against threats from within and without, love your neighbor. It seems obvious that we understand that The State is a sacred sphere because those who enter its service swear an oath to submit themselves in serving a cause ordained by One greater than themselves.

Now to the lie. A sphere loses its integrity when forces from another sphere begin to encroach on its sanctity. Another way to think of it is to blur the lines between one sphere and another. The State, because of the power vested in it and its vast wealth of resources, begins to see itself as god-like, having no boundaries and begins to assume control over the other spheres in the social order. Those serving as the authority of The State are human, flawed, subject to temptation, and aggrandizement of self. Thus, this sphere is easily corrupted and taken captive by the belief that it can function effectively without God.

The consequences of being taken captive by that lie can result in horrific suffering, as in the extreme examples of Hitler, Pol Pot, and Stalin. Overreach by The State need not be as egregious, as those examples, but it still creates confusion and conflict for those whose individual rights are being trampled. In America the sovereignty of the individual was intended to be sacrosanct.

In March 2010, *The Affordable Care Act*, better known as Obama Care, passed Congress by a highly contested 219-212 vote which was opposed by every single Republican. The document was some 2,300 pages and had not been widely read by members of Congress prior to the vote. Among the requirements of the law was the demand that health insurers cover comprehensive health care for women, including all methods of contraception and sterilization services. Coverage was based on recommendations by The Institute of Medicine and implemented by The Department of Health and Human Services.

Most people get health coverage through plans provided by their employers. Among employers are those whose services are faith-based enterprises. Among these are small organizations such as Little Sisters of the Poor, whose primary mission is to serve the needs of the elderly and the poor. So, here we have The State (Congress) poking its nose in the business of another sphere (Religion) by imposing a law that requires those covered by the integrity of that sphere to support the practice of abortion! Clearly a violation of a fundamental law of its own—The Little Sisters filed suit. It went all the way to Supreme Court.

On October 6, 2017, the Court unanimously overturned the lower courts that had ruled against the Little Sisters. The Court ordered the lower courts to accommodate the petitioners' religious beliefs. The consequences, of this unnecessary attempt to mandate a politicized social reform, include the cost of five years of litigation, emotional stress on nuns faced with a $75M annual fine for refusing to comply, and the time lost that could have been spent on administering to the elderly poor.

This is but a single example of The State usurping authority, blurring the line separating The State and freedom of religion. People of faith must remain vigilant, lest continued attacks on religious freedom become more flagrant. We should expect them to continue.

2. The Sovereignty of Marriage and Family
Regardless of what anyone, who in the name of tolerance or political correctness, says about the "virtue" of same-sex marriage, it stems from either ignorance of God's creation, naivete, or an outright lie. It has been accepted as fact from the beginning of mankind's history that the sphere of marriage has been consecrated, declared holy by Almighty God.

"God created man in His own image...male and female He created them. Then God blessed them, and God said to them, 'Be fruitful and multiply; fill the earth.'" (Genesis 1:27-28)

"Wives, submit yourselves to your own husbands as you do to the Lord. For the husband is the head of the wife as Christ is the head of the church, his body, of which he is the Savior. Now as the church submits to Christ, so also wives should submit to their husbands in everything. Husbands, love your wives just as Christ loved the church and gave himself up for her to make her holy, cleansing her by the washing with water through the word, and to present her to himself as a radiant church, without stain or wrinkle or any other blemish, but holy and blameless. (Ephesians 5:22-27)

This verse, no doubt, causes the extremists on the liberal left to go apoplectic. Submit! Women submit to your husbands! Never! You know I'm not exaggerating the liberals' response to something they likely don't understand. In today's politically correct (PC) world, there are words that have been twisted by the word police and social reformers who, without debate, want all things to match their worldview. *Submit*, as it's used in this context is a glorious word, a word of commitment and dedication out of pure love.

It has nothing to do with being a doormat or asking one to grovel for a scrap of bread. When Christ purchased his Church with his blood, paying the mortgage on the sin debt of all, he did so by submitting to the will of the Father. God loves us so much He asked His only son to bear a burden we cannot bear to redeem ourselves. This was the ultimate sacrifice, the unequaled submission of one for another. What greater statement of one's love and respect for another to say, I put your needs, your life before my own. I willingly lay down my life for you.

And that is what is being asked of the husband and wife, to willingly lay down his or her life in marriage, literally if necessary. Obviously, there was no Christian church prior to the Christ. He died to bring it to life, so that in his Church, in him, we can find eternal life.

In most cases, prior to marriage, a man is relatively free of the heavy commitments required by marriage and family. Once he becomes a husband, a man is called to love his wife, to serve and lead her in Godly ways, and present her without blemish. I take that to mean not to speak or act in any way that would discredit one's wife. To lie, to cheat on, or abuse his wife in any way, would dishonor and blemish her and the relationship. As a husband, a man has the opportunity in marriage and family to be Christ-like, by dying to self, he brings about abundant life to his family.

Let it be said, a man is not complete without a woman. *Then the* LORD *God said, "It is not good that the man should be alone; I will make him a helper fit for him."* (Genesis 2: 18)

And what kind of helper would be fit for a man? It would, of course, require a grand and glorious creature, an irresistible partner to make man complete. And this relationship is sacred. A husband protects his wife. She is a treasure he must keep without blemish. I think marriage is a profound mystery. A man and woman coming together to make one flesh, and yet, in a successful marriage, it happens. Two are transformed and become one—for better or worse. They make it work, and in that process, there is joy and humor. Joyous memories of family, and the goofiness and silly things that make us laugh at ourselves provide the stand-up comedians material for a lifetime.

"Let marriage be held in honor among all, and let the marriage bed be undefiled, for God will judge the sexually immoral and adulterous." (Hebrews13: 4)

"Do not be unequally yoked together with unbelievers. For what fellowship has righteousness with unrighteousness?" (2 Corinthians 6:14)

It must be clear to anyone with eyes to see and a mind to understand, that marriage and all that goes with it, was sanctified from the beginning by God. It is a natural sphere, sufficient within itself, and stands apart from socially organized spheres. *"But at the beginning of creation God 'made them male and female. For this reason, a man will leave his father and mother and be united to his wife, and the two will become one flesh. So they are no longer two, but one flesh. Therefore, what God has joined together, let no one separate."* (Matthew 19:4-6)

Obergefell et al. v. Hodges; U.S. Court of Appeals for the Sixth Circuit: On June 26, 2015, after a series of conflicting rulings from circuit courts at the state level, the Supreme Court ruled that state-level bans on same-sex marriage were unconstitutional, overturning all previous decisions to the contrary.

The Court examined the fundamental rights guaranteed by the due process clause and the equal protection clause of the *Fourteenth Amendment* of our *Constitution*. That ruling required all fifty states to allow same-sex couples to marry and grant them the same legal rights and responsibilities as between a man and woman. This is an ideal example illustrating what happens when man substitutes his wisdom for that of Almighty God. That which is ordained to be holy by the source of all Truth gets twisted into something that violates the integrity and law inherent in another sphere—marriage.

The Supreme Court as an agent of the State overstepped its authority in two major ways. One, by usurping the right of the individual states to decide whose law, God's or man's, they would choose to follow in defining marriage. Two (and without conscience), the Court granted itself the authority to redefine marriage, changing what should be understood as immutable, into a condition that violates the law of the religious sphere. Clearly a social sphere, the sovereignty of which was granted, from the beginning of human history, by the Creator alone.

Granted, the decision tickled the ears of the unbelievers; their references to the *Fourteenth Amendment* may be approved by those who are overwhelmed with the desire to ensure everyone *is* equal, not just equal under the law, but equal in every imaginable way. That's where the social reformers get off the tracks. The Court had to stand on its head to ensure the ruling fulfilled the agenda of the politically correct (PC) crowd.

Amendment XIV: Section 1: "All persons born or naturalized in the United States, and subject to the jurisdiction thereof are citizens...of the state wherein they reside. No state shall make or enforce any law which shall abridge the privileges and immunities of citizens..., nor shall any state deprive any person of life, liberty, or property, without due process of law; nor deny to any person within its jurisdiction the equal protection of the laws."

The Majority Opinion: Four reasons were given to support the right of same-sex couples to marry.

First, "The right to personal choice regarding marriage is inherent in the concept of individual." (Does that imply each of us gets to define marriage any way we'd like to have it?)

Second, "The right to marry is fundamental because it supports a two-person union unlike any other in its importance to the committed individuals, a principle applying equally to same-sex couples."

Third, "The fundamental right to marry safeguards children and families and thus draws meaning from related rights of childrearing, procreation, and education; as same-sex couples have children and families, they are deserving of this safeguard—though the right to marry in the United States has never been conditioned on procreation."

Fourth, "Marriage is a keystone of our social order, and there is no difference between same-and opposite-sex couples with respect to this principle; (That there is no difference becomes a factor only when the definition of marriage is changed to fit the condition. Author's opinion.) consequently, preventing same-sex couples from marrying puts them at odds with society, denies them countless benefits of marriage, and introduces instability into their relationships for no justifiable reason."

The Minority Opinion: The four dissenting judges made the following points.

First, the Court was cautioned, the due process clause has been misused in the past to expand <u>perceived</u> fundamental rights (author's emphasis), and that none of the previous rulings had changed the accepted definition of marriage, that it is a union between a man and a woman; therefore, the bans did not violate due process. (Only by changing the definition of marriage did the bans become unlawful.)

Second, the Court's decision effectively robbed the people of "the freedom to govern themselves." It shut down further public discussion, thereby establishing the judiciary as the primary decision maker rather than the democratic process which was the original intention. The *Constitution* does not authorize the Court to legislate.

Third, the only liberty protected under the due process clause is freedom from physical restraint. (The State can't lock a person up without due cause and process.) Liberty is understood to be an individual's freedom *from* government action (The State), not as a right *to* a specific entitlement. Think—marriage license or gun permit.

Fourth, the belief that same-sex marriage bestows dignity on anyone is false. Government isn't capable of giving dignity to anyone. Dignity is a natural right, an innate quality, a right that can't be denied even by slavery or internment camps! Furthermore, the majority's opinion could be used to attack the beliefs of those who disagree with same-sex marriage, putting them at risk of being labeled as bigots, treated as such by governments, employers, and schools. (We've already seen the evidence.)

Have we heard the last of this ruling? Austin Nimocks, senior counsel for the *Alliance Defending Freedom*, responded to the Court saying that "five lawyers took away the voices of more than 300 million Americans to continue to debate the most important social institution in the history of the world…Nobody has the right to say that a mom or a woman or a dad or a man is irrelevant. The *National Catholic Register* and *Christianity Today*, were among groups expressing concerns that there may be conflict between the ruling and religious liberty.

We're seeing the consequences of one sovereign sphere (The State) imposing its will on another—marriage, a religious institution. And so now the Court must decide, if same-sex marriage requires the owner of a bakery to violate his religious beliefs. If requested, is it unlawful for him to refuse to provide the couple with a wedding cake? God's laws are immutable. Those who are agents of the State and ignore their responsibility to protect the sovereignty of the other social spheres, do so at their own risk.

And before closing this segment, let's look at *Amendment XIV: Section 5*: "The Congress shall have the power to enforce, by appropriate legislation, the provisions of this article."

We recognize that at this point in America's turbulent history, our Congress is perceived as dysfunctional, bogged down in partisan politics. Would that it could muster the courage to stand up to the Supreme Court and challenge it to function within its prescribed role as interpreter of laws based on what is written in the *Constitution*, not what they personally believe should have been written. "Shoddy jurisprudence," Justice Clarence Thomas observed, "subverts the democratic process, and exalts judges at the expense of the People from whom they derive their authority."

Let's not forget, Christians are called to obey the laws established by the rulers, even when some are pressing against our core beliefs. We have permission to push back, gently with respect, and grounded in Truth.

3. Sovereignty of Religion (Worship). Can we use the words religion and worship interchangeably? No, but it's a relevant question, perhaps, central to the heart of this discussion regarding a nation divided. Follow me on this point. Let's begin with defining religion. Whoops, not as easy I thought. Philosophical, theological, and worldview arguments defining religion are wide and deep.

For the purpose at hand, I'm going to take the simple path and say, religion is a body of beliefs and practices associated with our human instinct that acknowledges the supernatural to explain our experiences in this world. The most fundamental practice of all religions is worship. Humans throughout history have worshipped. The deities we've chosen to worship represent a wide variety of possibilities, but we want to focus on the God of the *Holy Bible*, and freedom of religion in America.

We can believe in the God-given sovereignty of religion because God blessed the Jews as His people—The Chosen People. In Deuteronomy 6:1-25, following their release from bondage in Egypt, Moses spoke to his people about specific laws given to him by God on Mt. Sinai. Verses 23-25 clearly reveal God's intent for those laws to be that body of beliefs and practices, a religion, to fulfill His promises to their ancestors Abraham, Isaac, and Jacob.

> *"But he (God) brought us out from there (Egypt) to bring us in and give us the land he promised on oath to our ancestors. The LORD commanded us to obey all these decrees and to fear the LORD our God, so that we might always prosper and be kept alive, as is the case today. And if we are careful to obey all this law before the LORD our God, as he has commanded us, that will be our righteousness."*

That was the message approximately 3,500 years ago, some 1,500 years before Christ. It has been stated different ways, but Truth is at the mercy of those who control the media, or those with the greatest impact on the culture, or those who define the public narrative, or those with the sharpest sword. One of the ways to promote lies, then, is to control the message. If you say it enough times, loud enough, over a long enough period of time, even though the message is false, people will eventually believe it.

That concept illustrates the cosmic battle raging within the human community. Unbelievers are convinced that the origin of life, based on Darwin's hypothesis, is indisputable. They've held to that belief since 1859. That hypothesis has been stated long and loud by people in positions to control the message—it became accepted, not as a possibility, but fact. People believed and most stopped questioning its truthfulness.

Unbelievers remain skeptical of the trustworthiness of religions because religion requires, as some say, suspension of rational thought; there's no way to prove fanciful tales based in the supernatural. Believers, with great faith, have believed throughout the entire recorded history of mankind, the message that God or gods are present. Throughout the course of human history, that message, religion, has been challenged again and again.

Stick with me now; in America today, we're beginning to get signals that perhaps another message, a subtle lie, is being launched at the *First Amendment's* guarantee of religious freedom. Remember, worship is an essential element of the sovereign sphere of religion. Saying one has the freedom to worship, is not the same as saying we have freedom of religion.

Former President Obama and the Secretary of State, Hillary Clinton both, when speaking of religious freedom in America began to rephrase that basic right with the words, "freedom to worship." No big deal you say. I'm nit-picking or paranoid, or both. No. Words count, and if our leaders changed that phrasing intentionally, it is a big deal!

If a nation's leaders wanted to really scrub all references to anything religious from the public square, without using tanks or firing a shot, they would begin to use religion and worship interchangeably, over and over until maybe someone challenges the misstatement and asks for clarification. Lawsuits are filed, appeals follow, the matter goes before the Supreme Court. We just witnessed in the preceding discussion, that a majority of the Court, if necessary to get the "right" decision, is willing to change the definition of keywords (i.e., marriage).

Let's say the Court rules the words are in fact synonymous. So, now The State guarantees freedom to worship. Without the formality and political clout of the Church (organized religion), what is left of religion but an individual's right to worship in one's home? Preserving religion as a sovereign social sphere equal in relation to the sovereign sphere of The State, is critical to America's heritage of freedom from government. To maintain a free society, the sphere of The State must be restrained, monitored constantly, and reeled in when it oversteps its authority.

In 1788, James Madison, *Federalist 48,* wrote, "It will not be denied that power is of an encroaching nature and that it ought to be effectually restrained from passing the limits assigned to it."

Others among our Founding Fathers, shared Madison's concern that the federal government, with all powers invested in it, can easily usurp the power of its smaller units, thereby, violating a constitutional promise to the states, counties, municipalities, families, and individuals, the "unalienable right to life, liberty, and the pursuit of happiness."

Three years later, 1891, Congress addressed this concern by ratifying the *Bill of Rights,* thus affirming the intent to limit power at the federal level to ensure the rights of the states. The *Tenth Amendment* states: "The powers not delegated to the United States by the *Constitution,* nor prohibited by it to the states, are reserved to the states or to the people." *Article V* provides a means by which the states can amend the Constitution "when deemed necessary."

Common sense would dictate that individuals and families require the protection under the law of the State to defend their right to life and liberty. Happiness? It's not so clear. My first reaction is that government does not exist to guarantee my happiness.

Let's look at an example of the consequences that occur when the State blurs the line between its necessary power to legislate and its requirement to protect and defend the sovereignty of religious freedom.

On December 15, 2016, *The Indianapolis Star* reported that the town council of Knightstown, a small community about 40 miles east of the city, would be forced to remove a cross from atop a Christmas tree on the town square.

A single member of the community complained to the local *American Civil Liberties Union* (ACLU) that he didn't want his tax dollars going to support religion—citing the separation of church and state clause.

> *"Religious wars are not caused by the fact that there is more than one religion, but by the spirit of intolerance, the spread of which can only be regarded as the total eclipse of human reason."*
>
> de Montesquieu
>
> (1689-1755)

The town council submitted, citing lack of funds to fight the matter in court. The ACLU attorney said the removal of the display of the cross, a Christian symbol, has been ruled unconstitutional by the Supreme Court, and is a big victory in defense of the *First Amendment*. He further stated that his client "is very sincere" in his belief in the separation of church and state. He concluded, "People tend to think this is an attack on religion. All this is, is an effort to show the government does not have an establishment of religion."

Townspeople gathered to demonstrate in support of keeping the cross atop the tree. The pastor of the local Methodist Church led the rally. He told a *Star* reporter, "This is demonstrative of the erosion of free expression of religion. It's my hope in the future, someone would be able to put forward the case under the *First Amendment*, that such displays do not violate the establishment of the *First Amendment*."

I posed this question earlier regarding *Engle v. Vitale;* please explain to me, how in the world a simple prayer, or a cross, or any religious symbols, (A Star of David, a Dharma Wheel) displayed for public view equate with the establishment of a religion by the civil authority? If I happen to see that the local town board has displayed a Star and Crescent during Ramadan to acknowledge the Muslims living among us, I surely will not think, they've established Islam as our national religion! That is ridiculous!

> "A government big enough to give you everything you want is a government big enough to take from you everything you have."
>
> Gerald R. Ford, Pres., 1974-1977

Some PC extremist will wail and cry out, it might offend someone. Please, grow up. It is not the role of government to protect us from things we might find offensive. I repeat; that is not a function of government!

You'll recall, this discussion of six lies that have helped to divide America began with the "theory" of Darwinian evolution. Rapidly, it became an accepted fact, not theory, but scientific fact. We know that Darwin's "science" was based on observations being wildly extrapolated from noting changes in the size of birds' beaks to "theorize" that all living creatures have a common ancestry. (A "weak hypothesis" would have been a more appropriate label for that body of work.)

Beginning in roughly in the latter years of the 19th century, the accepted Truth of God was challenged by this "science." And, those who found the doctrine of the Church too restrictive, cramping their style, so to speak, used the doctrine of evolution to discredit religion and embrace a more convenient truth. There is no God, no need to worship, no need for religion.

The influence of religion remained stable until the war in Vietnam and the desegregation of public schools resulted in protests and violence, wracking America with spasms of divisive rhetoric, assassinations, and civil disorder. Dr. Martin Luther King was perhaps the last voice of spiritual leadership that could be heard above the fray, until silenced by an act of cowardly evil, April 4, 1968.

Since those tumultuous years, opinion polls reveal a slow but steady decline in two significant matters of religion. First, the number of people who identify with a religion has declined significantly, as has regular church attendance.

Second, the percent of adults who believe that religion has little or no relevance in their daily lives has increased significantly.

Now, let's back up just a bit. By the early 20th century, public schools had been established in more than half the states. In the late 19th century, John Dewey, the modern thinking progressive, you remember—the Father of American Education—was highly influential in establishing "modern" teaching, child-centered methods of instruction, including: experiential learning, doing projects of interest, grouping, and scientific methodology emphasizing math and science.

Sounds good in some ways, that as an educator, I would support. However, the point to be made is two-fold. First, you'll recall, Dewey perceived himself to be an intellectual, not requiring any trappings of God or religion to guide him. It was that belief that caused him to stumble spiritually. He bought the lie. Science teachers from that era on until today have been indoctrinated in the scientific "truth" of evolution. (Man arose from the goo.)

The second point is the consequence of the State, in the form of public education, exerting its powerful influence over millions and millions of children and young adults, over a period of more than a century. The sphere of the State with good intentions (always, it is the good intention) by teaching a godless science has intruded on the sanctity of two spheres: Marriage & family, and religion.

There is no way to assess the damage that has been done to our nation in the name of progressive education. As a public-school administrator for more than three decades, I ask you to consider this. Do you think the Unabomber, Ted Kaczynski, could have passed the *Scholastic Aptitude Test* (SAT)? He was a math prodigy, highly intelligent. He was also a domestic terrorist. Between 1978 and 1995, the man some considered a genius, killed three and severely injured others in 17 bombing episodes that kept our nation on edge.

Do you believe that Kenneth Lay, Ph. D. in economics, University of Houston, 1970, and Jeffrey Skilling, M.B.A., Harvard, 1979, the rich, well connected, and trusted executives at Enron, could have passed the SAT? They surely did, but that was before they "cooked the books" at Enron and victimized employee stockholders and hundreds of thousands of other investors who lost billions of dollars. What's the problem?

What about Bernie Madoff, former stockbroker, investment advisor, financier, and former non-executive chairman of the NASDAQ? Could he have passed the SAT? He was "smart" enough to make off with nearly $65 billion scammed from nearly 5,000 clients who admired and trusted him. He's in prison for life. What's the problem?

The problem is—pride, ego, thinking themselves as smarter, more entitled, above the law. They are examples of those who worship at the altar of secularism. Where there is no god, there is spiritual bankruptcy. Whether they attended public schools or private schools these men were aware of evolution as the source of life. Parents who perhaps never bought into that lie have had to battle confusion caused by progressive thinking. Despite being raised in homes that taught otherwise, children, teens, even young men and women of college age can be intimidated by educators, professors, who insist that Darwinism, as science, has removed all doubt about the origin of life.

The problem is—take God out of the equation and you can multiply the examples above by millions. "Good" men and women, intelligent people, high performers, well educated, seduced by the lie that their own sense of what is moral, what is ethical will suffice. It will not. What does one worship if it isn't God? Who does one serve if not God?

The State's extreme fear of religion's threat to the right to remain free of anything remotely religious, fails to recognize that when matters of the spirit are rejected, the values of paganism are by default, approved; therefore, the position of the Supreme Court is not neutral, as it piously likes to believe.

4. Sovereignty of Labor: We were born to create. You say, the title says labor; that sounds like work. You might be among many who see labor as something onerous, something wearisome, even oppressive. In looking at synonyms, I found: hard, exhausting, toilsome, great effort, physical (as in childbirth). I'll stick with the belief that labor is a God-given social sphere. Why? Because God labored for six days to create all that there is. God worked. He toiled, using His creativity, sense of beauty, order, inventiveness, and unparalleled integrated designs to produce paradise on earth and throughout the universe.

"In the beginning you laid the foundations of the earth, and the heavens are the work of your hands." (Psalm 102: 25)

"For in six days the L<small>ORD</small> *made the heavens and the earth, the sea, and all that is in them, but he rested on the seventh day. Therefore, the* L<small>ORD</small> *blessed the Sabbath day and made it holy."* (Exodus 20:11)

"The heavens declare the glory of God; the skies proclaim the work of his hands." (Psalm 19:1)

Of course, the "garden" shows significant signs of wear and tear resulting from our fall from grace. Never-the-less, God has modeled for us that work, the application of creative energy, skills to solve problems leading to the production of goods and materials, was intended to be a source of great joy and fulfillment. In this sphere, despite its fallen state, enough remains for us to see, as Dr. Del Tackett, *The Truth Project*, put it, "to serve as America's "engine room of culture." Without a workforce, society could not exist.

God's signature has been stamped on the sphere of labor. Remember, He has created us in His image, meaning that within us, some of His characteristics are embedded. Limited, yes, but we can see the relationships. God has given us the capacity to work. As sovereign over all, He blesses those who use their intelligence, imagination, effort, etc., to establish businesses that in turn, create jobs. Those employed to do the work generate goods and services required for society to flourish. But, you already knew that.

"You may say to yourself, "My power and the strength of my hands have produced this wealth for me." But remember the LORD your God, for it is he who gives you the ability to produce wealth, and so confirms his covenant, which he swore to your ancestors, as it is today." (Deuteronomy: 8:17-18)

Perhaps, what you haven't noticed is the triune nature of labor as we know it. God has established the system. Within the system, the business owner being established by God submits to God. That is, the owner acknowledges that he is serving God's purpose, and has a responsibility to treat employees accordingly. As we read in Matthew 20: 25-28, those in authority are not to lord it over people. They are to be good moral exemplars for those they serve. Thus, the owner submits to God.

Employees are called to submit to the will of the employer as God has instructed.

"Let everyone be subject to the governing authorities, for there is no authority except that which God has established. The authorities that exist have been established by God. Consequently, whoever rebels against the authority is rebelling against what God has instituted, and those who do so will bring judgment on

themselves. For rulers hold no terror for those who do right, but for those who do wrong. Do you want to be free from fear of the one in authority? Then do what is right and you will be commended. For the one in authority is God's servant for your good. But if you do wrong, be afraid, for rulers do not bear the sword for no reason. They are God's servants, agents of wrath to bring punishment on the wrongdoer. Therefore, it is necessary to submit to the authorities, not only because of possible punishment but also as a matter of conscience." (Romans 13: 1-7)

Thus, the employees submit to God and the owner. That three-way relationship of submission and accountability reflects the nature of God. (Father, Son, Holy Spirit). Those three elements united form one integrated whole, a single individual we call God.

In that relationship, we see God's divine imprint on the sphere of labor. God created the system. Owners operate the system within God's authority. Workers generate the goods and services that produce wealth. Three elements, God, owner, worker, united in a single integrated system. Wise owners return some of that wealth to the community to support public health, education, and the material needs of the people. It's not just the spirit of altruism; it's just good business.

" 'When you reap the harvest of your land, do not reap to the very edges of your field or gather the gleanings of your harvest. Leave them for the poor and for the foreigner residing among you. I am the Lord your God.' " (Leviticus 23:22)

Meeting material needs isn't the only function of labor; it includes those engaged in creative and performing arts. Music, for example, inspires and soothes the human soul. The artist's canvas and the photographer's eye capture images of reality and fantasy, interpreting the beauty and the horrors of our existence. In dance, drama, and films, bodies move, our imaginations are stirred. Poetry, literature, the story teller's lore, relating tales of love, jealousy, revenge, and adventure. Pottery, sculpture, jewelry, human hands fashioning, inventing designs the less talented cannot see. In this dimension of labor, personal satisfaction and spiritual fulfillment frequently walk hand in hand.

"From everyone who has been given much— much will be demanded; and from the one who has been entrusted with much, much more will be asked." (Luke 12:48)

I believe most Americans notice and appreciate the generous spirit of giving shown by some of our professional athletes by supporting humanitarian causes of their choice. They are given much—much! They have been given by their Creator the gift of exceptional athleticism in one or more of its various forms. They have been awarded outrageous salaries bordering on the obscene. Our labors are based on a free market economy. Those who entertain us are valued much—much higher than those who educate, serve, and protect. Freely they have been given. Freely they should give back, in humility and thanksgiving.

"Those who give to the poor will lack nothing, but those who close their eyes to them receive many curses." (Proverbs 28:27)

"Yours, LORD, is the kingdom; you are exalted as head over all. Wealth and honor come from you; you are the ruler of all things ... Everything comes from you, and

we have given you only what comes from your hand. (1 Chronicles 29:12-14)

The spheres of State, labor, and religion combine as a community to address the needs of those unable to work.

"The righteous care about justice for the poor, but the wicked have no such concern." (Proverbs 29:7)

"If anyone has material possessions and sees a brother or sister in need but has no pity on them, how can the love of God be in that person?" (1 John 3:17)

The verses above point to an essential truth about this matter of submission. When you read them in the context of modern secular America, and the nations-at-large over the past two and a half centuries, these verses describing the sphere of labor, require our attention.

Some of us surely struggle with the statement that the authorities have been established by God and those rebelling against those authorities bring judgment on themselves. History reveals there have been many brutal, unforgiving, Draconian, cruel rulers who have borne a terrible sword! It leaves some people with the belief that we are being told to submit to the most vile and evil beings that humanity can produce.

Clearly workers are not expected to give their support and allegiance to those who are not using God's playbook. *"I will not look with approval on anything that is vile. I hate what faithless people do; I will have no part in it."* (Psalm 101:3) This verse supports the belief that Christians are justified in resisting evil labor practices that would threaten the well-being of individuals or families. Let's look at the consequences that befall a society when the sovereign sphere of labor is punctured by outside forces.

On August 13, 2018, *The Indianapolis Star* featured an article by Holly Hays and Vic Ryckaert that serves as an example of the confusion that can result when the fundamental principles between sovereign spheres of labor and religion become blurred.

Basic facts of the report explained that a counselor at Roncalli High School had been placed on administrative leave when school officials learned that she was employed in violation of the terms of her contract.

Officials learned that the counselor was married to a woman, a clear violation of the terms established in the contract. Legal experts opined that the school authorities have the right to fire the employee who signed the contract knowing full well she must support the teachings of the Catholic church, including marriage "between a man and a woman," an expectation clearly defined in all the employees' contracts.

Roncalli is one of seven high schools in Marion county governed by the Archdiocese of Indianapolis. Its web page listed the K-12 enrollment to be nearly 24,000 students and more than 2,000 employees. The counselor had been employed for fifteen years and described by supporters as a "role model for students and a loyal employee." School officials were reluctant to speak to the issues for legal reasons and for the employee's privacy. However, the counselor said she had hired an attorney to represent her appeal.

The very next day, *The Star* began publishing letters to the editor. As you would expect, opinions were at opposite ends of the "fairness" continuum. On one hand, the "verdict is clear—guilty! She knowingly deceived her employer and the penalty is severe. She should be fired. The end!

On the other hand, it's the heartless hypocrisy of the Catholic church, the violation of non-discrimination laws, and the Archdiocese of Indianapolis that are at fault, needing to change their policies and rectify the injustice done to the employee. One writer asked, what would Jesus do? (Implying, I think, that all is forgiven, and the one who lied should be restored to her position.)

Another letter writer caught my attention, acknowledging that given the terms of the signed contract, she couldn't dispute the employee's guilt. She went on to say that she was "disgusted by the moral sickness" revealed by a church that historically has covered for sexual predators in its midst, while its teachings target a "happy, healthy" same-sex marriage." As a former Catholic, she wrote, "the twisted priorities revealed by this juxtaposition speak for themselves."

The sovereign sphere of religion, ordained by God, has a long history of internal missteps because those who administer in this sphere are flawed. It's not God's Word that is flawed; it's the people who apply it wrongly, by intent or out of ignorance. Either way, it's not the fault of the Creator. If we claim to be Christians, we're bound to the laws and teachings as recorded in the *Holy Bible*.

"Then the LORD God made a woman from the rib he had taken out of the man, and he brought her to the man. The man said, "This is now bone of my bones and flesh of my flesh; she shall be called 'woman,' for she was taken out of man." That is why a man leaves his father and

mother and is united to his wife, and they become one flesh." (Genesis: 2:22-24)

    It can't be made much clearer. God created woman to be man's mate (a partner, a counterpart) that would make a complete relationship—one flesh. In Ephesians 5:22-25, the apostle Paul explains the sacred nature of the relationship between a man and woman. He goes so far as to compare that relationship to Christ's sacrifice on the cross establishing the basis for the Church as Christians know it. Despite the ruling of the Supreme Court, it's my belief that the opinion of human judges does <u>not</u> change God's Word. You are free to believe whatever you choose. God has given you that right.

    The counselor's same-sex marriage violates what God has ordained. It's not up to me to judge her. She's an intelligent adult. She can make her own decisions. She is accountable in this instance to God and her employer. There appears to be no doubt that she lied to the administrators at Roncalli High School. Does that make her an evil person? No. None of us should dare "cast the first stone."

    The LGBTQ community is claiming foul, but their grievance is not directly relevant. The issue is not her sexual orientation. The employment contract of the Archdiocese (as noted in a letter submitted by Wendy P.) clearly states that all employees, Catholic or not, must abide by the teachings of the Catholic church. The issue is the blurring of the lines between the spheres of labor and religion. As an employee of the Archdiocese of Indianapolis, she signed a contract agreeing to the terms therein, which included specific reference to marriage as a union between a man and woman. This is the issue. All the other opinions that focus on the "stunning hypocrisy," The counselor as "a role model for students," and asking "what would Jesus do, distract from the deeper problem.

This case spotlights the problem for America. Two sovereign spheres of human endeavor—religion and labor advocating conflicting priorities. Labor laws require that equal opportunity prevails. Legal procedures are in place to guarantee that contracts and conditions prevent employers from using their superior negotiating power to take unfair advantage of employees or to discriminate in ways that are clearly unjust.

Religion, Christianity in this case, requires that the spiritual beliefs of the Catholic faith supersede those of labor. Why? Because it only makes common sense, and that is what frightens me. America is losing its capacity to exercise common sense. Redefining marriage is a prime example.

From a legal point of view, discrimination in terms of one's equal opportunity for employment based on sex, religion, race, or nationality has been effectively prohibited by *Title VII, Civil Rights Act of 1964. However,* the Court did make one important exception—religion. Thankfully, in this matter, the Court applied common sense and appeared to acknowledge the sovereignty of the religious sphere.

It was recognized that the unique role of religion was forever (hopefully) protected in America by the *First Amendment* of our *Constitution*. "Congress shall make no law respecting an establishment of religion or prohibiting the free exercise thereof." Therefore, this law trumps any attempt by government (The State) to dictate policy to religious organizations.

Religious organizations by their very nature are discriminatory. Either you believe there is a God or gods, or you don't. Common sense tells us that if the State has the authority to dictate policy in matters of religious beliefs or activities, it has overreached. It would signal the end of the religious liberty in America. (By the way, since there are only two choices, if you choose to be an unbeliever, aren't you discriminating?)

Common sense dictates that a Catholic school would want to hire only those who subscribe to the teachings of the Catholic church. Would we really expect to find an atheist teaching history at Roncalli High School? That's not a slam at atheists, it's simply a fact—they do not meet the requirements of the employer. The exception to the *Civil Rights Act (1964)* includes all employees of a religious organization, not just those in administrative positions.

Some supporters believe the counselor should be reinstated because she's a "loyal" employee. Loyal employees don't deceive their employer. Others side with her because she's a "role model" for students. She may be perceived as such by many, but the case has been made that guidance counselors as role models don't deceive. To say this is not a condemnation of the woman in question; it is but to acknowledge that she stumbled. No one tripped her. She alone stands accountable for her choices, as do we all.

Regarding the opinion writer's question: What would Jesus do? That' a good question. Let's go to the source and see what he might have to say. Several opinions published in *The Star* cited the verse, *"Jesus said, Go and sin no more."* (John 8:11) Let's put those words in the context in which they were spoken. A woman caught in the act of adultery was brought to Jesus by her accusers thinking he would condemn her sin and they would be justified in executing her by stoning. He wrote something in the dirt. We don't know what he wrote, but by asking, *"Who will cast the first stone?"* Her accusers dropped the case and left the scene, leaving Jesus alone with the woman.

He did not condemn her. Does that mean he condoned her sin? Of course not. Who was harmed? Some scholars believe she was likely a prostitute. Her sinful lifestyle was of greater harm to her than anyone else. Sin impairs our relationship with God. It causes distress in all kinds of ways harmful to individuals and to others as well. Perhaps Jesus told her to go and sin no more because he cared about her and wanted what was best for her—give up her sinful lifestyle.

That Jesus loves us is not to be disputed. But Jesus is a tough guy. He stood face to face with men determined to find justification for killing him and called them hypocrites, fools, and vipers. He took a whip and drove the money changers from the Temple. He endured a merciless beating and died an excruciating death. Don't believe that he takes sin lightly and lets us off the hook.

The Parable of Talents (Matthew 25:14-30) is a testimony to the fact that we are held accountable. The man who failed to wisely invest the talent he was given was cast out. This parable is about how we employ our spiritual gifts, working for God's glory. Sometimes, for our benefit, Jesus exercises tough love! Holding us accountable when we mess up, just as any good friend would do. So, with respect to what Jesus would say, I don't know. Many times when we look back at the "bad" things that have befallen us, we find that they were blessings in disguise. If the Roncalli counselor humbly regrets that she stumbled, perhaps she'll find another job even more fulfilling than the one she has forfeited. God moves in mysterious ways.

Jesus didn't condemn (seek to punish) the adulteress. It's very unlikely that Roncalli will condemn the counselor. Among the options given her, only dissolving the marriage could be, in any way, considered as punitive. Getting fired, resignation, or non-renewal of a contract aren't punishments. They are natural consequences resulting from her wrongful action. Punishment would perhaps be requiring her to repay the employer for the time she worked in violation of her contract. Maybe her employers will simply say, go and sin no more.

Regardless, of the outcome, this anecdote serves to inform us of the difficult, but essential task of respecting and maintaining sphere sovereignty as a cornerstone in the foundation of our democracy.

On a larger scale, we can heed the case of *King et al. v. Burwell, Secretary of Health and Human Services, et al. Certiorari to the United States Court of Appeals for the Fourth Circuit.* (*www.supremecourt.gov/opinions/14pdf/14-114_qol1.pdf*)

On June 25, 2015, Supreme Court Chief Justice, John Roberts, issued the majority opinion deciding the matter of *King v. Burwell* making the *Patient Protection and Affordable Care Act,* (Obama Care) the law of the land. As we noted earlier, in the suit filed by the Little Sisters of the Poor, health care reform was, and remains, an issue that divides our nation. Obviously, the ruling favored the proposed health care plan, even though it was so poorly written, the Court concluded it had the authority to determine the correct meaning of certain parts of the document that, when read, appeared self-contradictory.

The decision of the Court to grant itself the authority rule based on its interpretation of what lawmakers meant to say, rather than interpret the law as written should be of concern to all Americans regardless of politics! It is not within the parameters of the Court's power to rewrite laws; that function has been clearly given to Congress!

Let's examine a few of the arguments put forth by Justice Antonin Scalia, who wrote the minority opinion, raising many questions and calling out the Court for its flagrant abuse of authority. He begins by identifying one of the elements in the document that encouraged confusion.

> "The Court holds that when the Patient Protection and Affordable Care Act says, 'Exchange established by the State' it means 'Exchange established by the State or the Federal Government.' That is of course quite absurd, and the Court's 21 pages of explanation make it no less so."

> "It provides, among other things, that every State 'shall ... establish an American Health Benefit Exchange'—a marketplace where people can shop for health-insurance plans. And ... if a State does not comply with this instruction, the Secretary of Health and Human Services must 'establish and operate such Exchange within the State.'"

He's making clear that the legislation as written says nothing about the federal government having any role in the proposed process. It was the Court majority that decided that it was obvious the authors <u>meant to say,</u> "Federal Government."

It was argued that this was simply an error in transcription. If so, then the same error was repeated in seven separate places when referring to tax credits. You would think the editors would catch at least one of seven miscues. Justice Scalia went on to point out:

> "This case requires us to decide whether someone who buys insurance on an Exchange established by the Secretary of Health and Human Services gets tax credits. You would think the answer would be obvious—so obvious there would hardly be a need for the Supreme Court to hear a case about it. To receive (coverage), an individual must enroll in an insurance plan through an 'Exchange established by the State.' The Secretary of Health and Human Services is not a State. So an Exchange established by the Secretary is not an Exchange established by the State—which means people who buy health insurance through such an Exchange get no money (coverage)."

In my humble mind, these are clearly valid arguments revealing how sorely flawed this law was as originally written. The majority justices had to use the power of their own pens to amend the law. Let's return to Scalia's observations. As one example to reveal the befuddling language, he wrote:

> "Words no longer have meaning if an 'Exchange that is *not* established by a State is 'established by the State.'"

> If you read that sentence within the context of a document, would you not be confused?

Justice Scalia cited other examples of confounding language requiring the Court to "clarify" the intent. If the intent is not clear, it can't be left to the Court to decide what the authors should have written. He stated:

> "The plain, obvious, and rational meaning of a statute is always to be preferred to anything curious, narrow, hidden ..., in short, the Government should lose this case. But normal rules of interpretation seem always to yield to the overriding principle of the present Court: The Affordable Care Act must be saved."

Justice Scalia goes on to chastise the Court for its attempts to correct flawed and poorly written legislation. At one point he referred to the Court's desire to save the bill by "interpretive jiggery-pokey."

> "The Court's decision reflects the philosophy that judges should endure whatever interpretive distortions it takes in order to correct a supposed flaw in the statutory machinery. That philosophy ignores the American people's decision to give Congress 'all legislative Powers' enumerated in the Constitution. Art. I, §1. They made Congress, not this Court, responsible for both making laws and mending them. This Court holds only the judicial power—the power to pronounce the law as Congress has enacted it. We lack the prerogative to repair laws that do not work out in practice, just as the people lack the ability to throw us out of office if they dislike the solutions we concoct. We must always remember, therefore, that 'our task is to apply the text, not to improve upon it.'"

Justice Scalia continued to reveal the lack of thoughtful deliberation and quality that went into the Affordable Care Act. He reinforced the fact that it isn't the place of the Court to "make everything come out right when Congress does not do its job properly." When Congress fails to act with competence, it's up to the people to hold them accountable. He wrote, "Rather than rewriting the law under the pretense of interpreting it, the Court should have left it to Congress to decide what to do."

Following are excerpts from the last two paragraphs of the dissenting opinion. Scalia's words should enrage those who believe in the sanctity of the Supreme Court of the United States. By so outrageously overstepping their authority, the liberal justices are soiling the reputation of the Court. The legislative and executive branches of our government must reign them in.

"Just ponder the significance of the Court's decision to take matters into its own hands. The Court's revision of the law authorizes the Internal Revenue Service to spend tens of billions of dollars every year in tax credits ... It affects the price of insurance for millions of Americans, ... diminishes the participation of the States in the implementation of the Act ... vastly expands the reach of the Act's individual mandate ... What a parody today's decision makes of Hamilton's assurances to the people of New York: 'The legislature not only commands the purse but prescribes the rules by which the duties and rights of every citizen are to be regulated. The judiciary, on the contrary, has no influence over ... the purse; no direction ... of the wealth of society, and, can take no active resolution whatever. It may truly be said to have neither force nor will but merely judgment." The Federalist No. 78, p. 465 (C. Rossiter ed. 1961).

Justice Scalia concluded:

"Perhaps the Patient Protection and Affordable Care Act will attain the enduring status of the Social Security Act or the Taft-Hartley Act; perhaps not. But this Court's two decisions on the Act will surely be remembered through the years. The somersaults of statutory interpretation they have performed ... publish forever the discouraging truth that the Supreme Court of the United States favors some laws over others, and is prepared to do whatever it takes to uphold and assist its favorites ... I dissent."

This decision by our Supreme Court shows the confusion that results when one sovereign sphere (Government as represented by the Court) interferes with the internal integrity of other sovereign spheres (in this instance labor, states' rights, and individual liberty). Not only that, but this case brings to light that our Forefathers understood the concept of sovereignty, and, attempted to guarantee it in the design of our *Constitution*. Three sovereign branches, equal in status and independence, were given clearly defined authority to act in behalf of the People.

In deciding and reinventing *Obama Care*, the Supreme Court in violation of the concept of sovereignty:

First, usurped the power of Congress to write and amend statutes.

Second, it bypassed the authority of Congress to allocate funds and implement the law.

Third, trampled on the rights of the individual states to regulate commerce.

Fourth, it violated the sphere of labor by placing illegal mandates on businesses.

Fifth, it violated the rights of individual citizens by requiring them to purchase insurance under penalty of the law. The mandate to purchase was re-labeled a tax.

The vote was 6-3. Six individuals in black robes allowed their personal bias to supersede their ability to objectively remain within the boundaries of their own sphere. Dangerous.

Nancy Pelosi (D)

House Minority Leader

Photo: (https://longroom.com/54591)

"But we have to pass the bill so that you can find out what is in it— away from the fog of the controversy."

A speech at the 2010 Legislative Conference for the National Association of Counties, 9 March 2010

5. Sovereignty of the Fourth Estate: Surely, we can agree on the essential role of an independent press and media in objectively reporting the words and actions of those who govern. In the absence of photographers, journalists, and investigative reporters, who are at the heart of this sovereign sphere, our nation would be the mercy of those who rule.

Imperfect as it is, the Fourth Estate is the wall that divides and protects. "The pen is mightier than the sword," familiar words by English author Edward Bulwer-Lytton, 1839.

Brave men and women risk their lives at home and abroad to get access to newsworthy events that we rely on as citizens. They are the messengers, keeping us informed of things that, otherwise, we'd never know or understand. Bearing the news has always been a dangerous lot.

> "As a conservative who believes in limited government, I believe the only check on government power in real time is a free and independent press. A free press ensures the flow of information to the public, and let me say, during a time when the role of government in our lives and in our enterprises seems to grow every day--both at home and abroad - ensuring the vitality of a free and independent press is more important than ever."
>
> Mike Pence, Vice President, 2017 –
>
> *brainyquote.com/quotes/mike pence*

"Lord, they have killed your prophets, they have torn down your altars, and I alone am left, and they are seeking my life." (1 Kings 19:10-14)

Elijah knew the reality of emperors that did not want to receive any bad news for fear the people would learn the truth and rebel. We bear witness to the fact that some things never change. Under dictatorships, there is no sovereignty of the press. In America, from the earliest days of the republic, our elected leaders have frequently complained about, been at odds with, the nation's press corps. However, none would dare seriously propose interfering with the sovereignty of a free and independent press.

Fourth Estate sovereignty can be threatened and has been corrupted from time to time—bribery and special interests being the prime culprits. News outlets and publishers with bias are commonplace. For example, most Americans will recognize that conservative political views are favored by *Fox News, the Drudge Report, Rush Limbaugh,* and *the Wall Street Journal.* Liberal politics will be favored by *The Washington Post, The New York Times, MSNBC*, and *The Guardian.* However, sophisticated hackers, national and international, threaten the sovereignty of this sphere. When consumers can't determine the true identity of the owner/publishers, Russian, Chinese, Iranian maybe—who can we believe?

So, the press and media, act as the "watchman" for us, but who watches the watchman? In the final analysis, We the People, are charged with keeping our collective eyes and ears open watching for signs of corruption, decay, and deceit within the sphere of the Fourth Estate. A single person or an alert organization can take down the wicked among the reporters and the false prophets.

A case in point, on May 28, 1985, President Ronald Reagan delivered a message from the Oval Office; he spoke to the nation calling for tax reform. The Democrats

had selected Dan Rostenkowski, a career politician from Chicago, who had risen through party ranks to become chairman of the Ways and Means Committee, as the one to deliver the televised response.
(http//www.enwikipedia.org/wiki/Dan_Rostenkowski)

  Rostenkowski spoke briefly to the point, appealing to the common sense of the working class. His remarks focused on reasons why people have lost faith in the tax system. Why should the teller pay higher taxes than the bank? Why does the gas station attendant pay a higher share than the oil company he works for? He made it clear that fair and simple taxes for individuals and businesses was a "historic Democratic commitment." In closing, he asked viewers to write him showing their support. He received more than 75,000 letters.

  As a result, President Reagan asked House Republicans to support the tax-revision bill drafted by the House Ways and Means Committee led by Rostenkowski, "While the proposals ... are far from perfect, Reagan observed, "they do represent a tax code that is fairer, simpler and encourages greater growth," Big win for Rosty.

  A grand success story began, but seven years later, it took a wrong turn. In December 1992, the *Chicago Sun-Times* headline read: "Rosty's Phantom Office." The story told readers how Rostenkowski had accepted money from his campaign committee to rent office space in a building owned by him and his sister. The space amounted to little more than a mail drop, but he was earning $1,250 a month on the vacant space.

  The web of corruption was beginning to unravel. A month later, the *Sun-Times* reported that he had appropriated more than $68,000 in taxpayer's money to lease three automobiles that later became Rostenkowski's personal property. A grand jury subpoenaed his auto records.

On June 1, 1994, Pierre Thomas, *The Washington Post* reported that a federal grand jury had charged Rostenkowski with misappropriating more than a half-million dollars, tampering with a witness and "using taxpayers' money to enrich himself, his friends and his family." In all, Thomas reported, 17 felony counts were filed including: mail & wire fraud, obstruction of justice, embezzlement, concealment and conspiracy.

A public servant, a man one friend described as "a larger than life figure, like some Shakespearean figure, a noble man with a tragic flaw. It's not like this is an evil man we're dealing with here. He gives thousands of dollars to charities. He's a good congressman. He just has some human frailties."

April 9, 1996, David E. Rosenbaum reported for *The New York Times*, that Rostenkowski had pleaded guilty to two charges of mail fraud and would serve a prison sentence of 17 months. The congressman was quoted as saying he had behaved no differently from most other members of Congress.

Now think about this; this is a man elected as a public official (to serve and protect), rises to become chair of the *House Ways and Means Committee*, is charged with 17 felony counts, cops a plea, does 17 months at a federal prison in Oxford, WI, and said his behavior was no different than most other members of Congress. Wow!

"Rosty," wielded financial power and influence in our nation's capital for over thirty years. He also appears to have embezzled, obstructed, concealed and conspired. He was removed from power because of articles first printed in the *Chicago Sun-Times*. The Fourth Estate punctured the sovereignty of the State, drained a drip from the swamp, and accomplished what Congress was likely to have ignored.

"These are the things which you should do: speak the truth to one another; judge with truth and judgment for peace in your gates. 'Also let none of you devise evil in your heart against another, and do not love perjury; for all these are what I hate,' declares the LORD." (Zechariah 8:16-17)

The Miami Herald columnist, Leonard Pitts, noted that the nation's press corps is the only profession protected by name in the *Constitution*. The July 8, 2018, article focused on his concern that given the current hyper-level of vitriol coming from extremists at both ends of the liberal/conservative continuum, someone is going to get hurt. As a case in point, Pitts pointed to the recent murder of five staffers at the Annapolis *Capital Gazette*. An emotionally unstable individual took deadly revenge on those with whom he held a grievance.

> *"I would rather have a free press without a government, than a government without a free press."*
>
> Thomas Jefferson

Given President Trump's non-stop criticism of the press and media for manufacturing fake news, and some criticism is clearly justified, but accusing the entire profession, is itself fake news. Not all are guilty, but all are beginning to feel on edge. Someone is going to get hurt. Mr. President, please, consider the unintended consequences.

As in all human endeavors, professionals included, there are those who fall victim to the lie and begin to believe they are above the law. Journalists are not immune. Dan Rather, formerly with *CBS* news, pushed the envelope too far trying to discredit President George W. Bush's military service. Brian Williams, former *NBC* news anchor, lied to his audience about surviving a helicopter crash shot down while covering the war in Iraq. *MSNBC*'s Rachel Maddow accused conservative talk show host, Rush Limbaugh of racism, citing "remarks" he made questioning then president Obama's birth certificate. She was forced to apologize to Limbaugh for intentionally lying for political gain

These examples are not intended to smear those cited, but to acknowledge that even among those who are respected, award winning reporters, none are immune to the temptation to put themselves above those they serve. The sovereignty of the Fourth Estate is entrusted to men and women who, risking life and limb, go willingly into danger, to learn and report the truth.

In 2002, Daniel Pearl a journalist for *The Wall Street Journal* was kidnapped in Pakistan by members of Al Qaeda. Later the civilized world was repulsed by a terrorist propaganda video showing Pearl's beheading by Khalid Sheikh Mohammed.

In 2005, men driving a police car abducted freelance journalist Steven Vincent and his interpreter from a street in Basra, Iraq. Vincent, a contributor to *The Christian Science Monitor* and *National Review,* referred to himself as "a soldier with a pen." Perhaps his stories revealed too much of the ugly side of Basra. Later, his body riddled with bullets, his hands bound with plastic wire was found thrown from a car. The interpreter survived.
(https://www.americanthinker.com/articles/2015/08/steven_vincent_insightful_war_reporter_murdered_in_iraq_ten_years_ago.html)

On November 22, 2012, freelance journalist James Foley, disappeared near the Turkish border of Syria. He had been reporting for various media outlets including *Agence France-Presse* and *Global Post*. Later, a gruesome video surfaced showing graphic images of his beheading by ISIS terrorists. (https://www.cnn.com/2014/08/19/world/meast/isis-james-foley/index.html)

These three examples are not meant to sensationalize violence, but rather serve as a reminder that since 1992, 880 journalists representing countries around the globe have been killed. The data collected and confirmed by the *Committee to Protect Journalists* (CPJ) shows that reporters are increasingly at risk. Iraq and Pakistan pose the greatest danger for journalists. (https://www.theguardian.com/datablog)

The point is this. The integrity of the Fourth Estate rests with those within its sovereign circle. We depend on them to provide dependable, objective reporting of the facts. Editors, for the press and media corps, its heroes and villains, must keep opinions from creeping into its news stories; assign opinions to the editorial and opinion pages— we count on honesty. Tell the truth. If you want to spin the story in favor of your bias, fine. Just don't be guilty of reporting "fake news!" America cannot afford to have the sovereignty of the press and media corrupted by politics!

"Keep watch over yourselves and all the flock ... savage wolves will come in among you and will not spare the flock ... Even from your own number men will arise and distort the truth to draw away disciples after them." (Acts 20: 28-30)

Part Three

Religion on Trial

"We have staked the future of all our political institutions upon the capacity of each and all of us to govern ourselves, to control ourselves, to sustain ourselves according to the Ten Commandments of God."

James Madison, *Father of the Constitution of the United States*

Religion or Humanism:
How Shall Christians Testify?

We began *Part One* with the premise that America is divided. In a diverse society, that's to be expected. Being divided is not a bad thing; it even works to our advantage in the form of competition. Disagreement challenges our thinking, fuels creativity, encourages problem-solving, and presents an array of options from which to choose. By and large, most things that divide us are relatively harmless: Yankees or Dodgers, Chardonnay or Merlot, pepperoni or veggie, Eastwood or Spike Lee, Ford or Chevy. These preferences are the basis for good-natured rivalries among friends and within families. How dull life would be without them.

https://pastordanielcox.co

At the other end of the continuum are issues related to politics, gun control, civil rights, right to life, race/ethnicity, immigration, freedom of expression, and you can add to the list. These matters are fundamental to maintaining social order. Because they affect all citizens, the manner by which government implements its policies, creates an emotionally charged set of conditions that invariably favor one group over another.

Of the issues that confront America, we have stated the single most divisive is one's worldview, the mental model that explains how things work in this world.

Do you believe the universe is the result of a random process having no purpose beyond its own existence? Or, do you believe there is evidence that points to a Creator, a supernatural being, that we call God, who has brought all things in to existence and has revealed Himself to us through the *Holy Bible* and by the physical laws that govern the awesome power and beauty of the universe?

These two views are mutually exclusive. You can't believe both at the same time. As a Christian, I believe Jesus is real. The Son of God, he lived among us, taught us how to live; we rejected him and his teaching—too radical. He was subjected to torture, humiliation, and was executed by crucifixion, fulfilling the prophesy that God would send a Messiah who would be sacrificed as atonement for the sins of ALL mankind.

"Surely he took up our pain and bore our suffering, yet we considered him punished by God, stricken by him, and afflicted. But he was pierced for our transgressions, he was crushed for our iniquities; the punishment that brought us peace was on him, and by his wounds we are healed. We all, like sheep, have gone astray, each of us has turned to our own way; and the LORD *has laid on him the iniquity of us all."* (Isaiah 53:4-6)

He punched a ticket for all of us. As color commentator, Bob Cook, used to exclaim when coming on the air for Indiana University basketball, "I've got my ticket; have you got yours?!" I'm not making light of his sacrifice; I'm calling to you. If you haven't responded to

Jesus' invitation to accept him as your personal Lord and Savior, please give it serious consideration. It's the most important decision you'll ever make. Don't blow it.

In *Part I*, we emphasized the consequences of our fallen state. America has largely turned its back to the reality of sin. Sin is not a popular word and as a nation we've become so emotionally fragile, some choose to ignore the Truth about the human condition—none are righteous. None. Rather than acknowledging their transgressions, many are choosing to substitute a distorted view of tolerance to excuse immorality. Having been taught only the good news that God loves us; therefore, all is forgiven. They believe sin is no big deal. Not so.

We're living in a time when those who profess to be Christians, believing they are true disciples of Jesus, will have their faith sorely tested. Those with a secular worldview are gaining momentum. Their numbers are growing. At the same time, as we've cited more than once, the number of Americans holding to a Christian, or another religious worldview, is declining. More and more we're seeing the consequences that result when the laws of man are clearly favored over the Truth of God. Scripture has foretold this.

"But mark this: There will be terrible times in the last days. People will be lovers of themselves, lovers of money, boastful, proud, abusive, disobedient to their parents, ungrateful, unholy, without love, unforgiving, slanderous, without self-control, brutal, not lovers of the good, treacherous, rash, conceited, lovers of pleasure rather than lovers of God— having a form of godliness but denying its power. Have nothing to do with such people." (2 Timothy 1-5)

Whether we're near end times, who can say, but the adjectives seem appropriate for describing contemporary America. Suicide is on the increase, abortion, alcoholism, pornography, sex trafficking, divorce, mass murders, an opioid epidemic, progressive public schools encourage socialism, hateful speech stifles debate, our national debt is beyond absurd, political gridlock rules Washington—our beloved America is in trouble. Three of every four adults believe we're on the wrong path, but we don't agree on which path to follow.

Being able to discern what is true is being confounded by the 24/7/365 "breaking news" cycle that has been corrupted by unprecedented exaggeration, allegations, and innuendos of wrong doing reported as fact from anonymous sources, and outright expressions of hate directed at the President, his family, and all who support him. It has reached a point where the public doesn't know who can be trusted to report without giving the news a partisan spin or relying on claims of the "anonymous."

Emotional arguments, abusive verbal bullying, fan the fires of violence. The result is chaos; the tempered voice of reason has become a whisper. Secular humanism and socialism are diametrically opposed to the beliefs upon which our nation was founded, but these philosophies are gaining support, especially among younger voters who have been indoctrinated by humanist propaganda, that over the past half-century has dominated public schools. Instruction in any other worldview is unlawful.

A 2017 Gallup poll reported that fifty-five percent of 18-29 years old's have a "positive view of socialism. *YouGov.com* recently reported forty-four percent of millennials would favor living in a socialist country as opposed to a capitalist nation such as America. That should sound the alarm.

Religion has become the enemy of government. The sanctity of marriage as ordained by God has been discarded in favor of a new definition written by five lawyers in black robes. The lives of the unborn can be snuffed out because they're an inconvenience. Individuals are elevated, idolized as saintly, because they're confused about their sexuality. Leaders in the highest offices of government, the Church, the military, and media have lied to us so often we've become indifferent to it. As these issues increase in frequency and intensity, Christians will be challenged to take a stand. Do we really believe that what we believe is really real? Those who are lukewarm will be at risk.

Jesus said, "But since you are like lukewarm water, neither hot nor cold, I will spit you out of my mouth!" (Revelation 3:16)

The denial of God's commandments has led to morality by majority opinion. If fifty-one percent of the population agree same-sex marriage or shacking-up are acceptable standards for marriage, those popular beliefs are adopted as the moral standard. Convenient, is it not, that society by majority rule gets to define what is moral? As has often been cited, just because it's legal doesn't make it right. In a society turned upside down, the cry for tolerance has been replaced by shrieks of intolerance.

In *Part Two*, we put forth six examples of lies that in less than a single century twisted America, like twisting a wash rag, two separate ends, two worldviews, with a tight knot in the middle that blocks the flow of civil discourse and debate. The consequences have poisoned our sense of unity—"One nation under God, with liberty and justice for all."

In 1859, the bible of evolution, *On the Origin of Species*, by Charles Darwin was published. Millions were influenced because his theory was adopted and promoted as fact by intellectuals, humanists and socialists in powerful positions, especially education. They believed it answered the question: Are we children of God or the goo?

Modern science has clearly revealed what Darwin could not have known. The odds that life, as we know it, do not support Darwin's theory that it evolved over eons of time as the result of random processes, without any meaningful purpose. It remains unlawful in our public schools to teach any worldview that suggests otherwise. If there is no God, life is but a cruel accident.

In December of 1953, the first edition of *Playboy* hit the newsstand. It was 44 pages, no date on the cover because Hugh Hefner wasn't sure there would be a second edition! However, the centerfold of Marilyn Monroe was enough. He sold 54,175 copies, 50 cents a copy. Slick packaging and airbrushed nudity enabled Hefner to repackage pornography as a clean, wholesome version, of what had been socially taboo, a closet enterprise, shunned in polite circles.

What followed were copy-cat versions without the airbrushed images and "scholarly" articles featuring art, music, philosophy, and politics. *Hustler, Penthouse, and Gent* went over the top. Rude, crude, and without pretense of presenting sexuality as anything glamourous—raw, down & dirty to the core. The exploitation and abuse of women. The internet has only made it worse. If you're at all in touch with the headlines, well-known men of nearly every profession have been identified as sexual predators. That pornography is not a serious social problem in America is to believe a lie.

In 1963, because of the liberal, socialist agenda of Madalyn Murray O'Hair, Chief Justice of the Supreme Court, Earl Warren, handed down an 8-1 decision declaring that "reading scripture and reciting the Lord's Prayer are devotional, religious observances." Thus, God was expelled from the nation's public schools.

Many educators who were my colleagues at that time, believe that discipline, respect, and accountability in public schools have gone down largely because there is no consistent moral authority among the stakeholders. Millions of students have been deprived of the right to evaluate the truth of the socialist humanist manifesto.

The Pentagon Papers, commissioned in 1967, is an official account of America's policies and objectives related to the Vietnam war. The stunning lies of four presidents, a Secretary of Defense, field generals, and other federal officials have had a lasting effect on our country.

Perhaps we were naive to believe that our elected officials and military personnel at the highest level would never blatantly lie to us, hiding their own incompetence while protecting their professional careers. Their collective arrogance and pride contributed greatly to the prolonged conflict that cost 58,318 American lives. The divisiveness and disillusionment caused by that war haunt us yet today.

Daniel Ellsberg served as a platoon leader and company commander in the 2nd Marine Division; he blew the whistle bringing the lies to light on the pages of the *Pentagon Papers*. However, he was charged as a traitor facing charges carrying a total maximum sentence of 115 years under the *Espionage Act of 1917*. A trial began in Los Angeles on January 3, 1973. On May 11, all charges were dismissed when it was learned that the *Watergate* scandal made clear that his actions were in fact those of a patriot. It takes good ol' fashioned guts to call out liars in high places, knowing they have the power and influence to silence you—permanently.

On January 22, 1973, the Supreme Court of the United States issued its 7-2 decision favoring the plaintiff, Roe, overturning an earlier interpretation of abortion rights by a Texas court. The fundamental question before the Court was when does life begin. Scientists and doctors had established no formal consensus regarding that matter. Testimonials by those qualified to speak, agreed that biologically, life begins at the moment of conception. However, a second question was raised. When does a life become a functional human?

> Justice Harry Blackmun wrote: "Texas urges that, apart from the Fourteenth Amendment, life begins at conception … is present throughout pregnancy, …, therefore, the State has a compelling interest in protecting that life from and after conception. We need not resolve the difficult question of when life begins. When those trained in the respective disciplines of medicine, philosophy, and theology are unable to arrive at any consensus, the judiciary, at this point in the development of man's knowledge, is not in a position to speculate."
> (web.utk.edu/~mfitzge1/docs/374/Blackmun_Roe.pdf. Blackmun opinion of the Court in Roe v Wade 1973 p.16)

The decision was loudly proclaimed as a victory for a woman's right to choose whether to deliver or abort a human life. This is the result when mankind decides what is politically expedient, allowing God's authority to be set aside in favor of human desires—the right to choose one's own desire at the expense of another.

"See now that I myself am He! There is no god besides me. I put to death and I bring to life, I have wounded and I will heal, and no one can deliver out of my hand." (Deuteronomy 32:39)

It's so tempting to use our free will option to play god when God's word would prevent us from getting our own way. Who speaks for those who cannot speak for themselves? To deny that a human life begins at conception is to succumb to a lie.

Sphere sovereignty, an unfamiliar concept to many, is the belief that there are certain areas of human endeavor, sanctified by God and if properly observed help to maintain the balance among the rights of individuals, those of religion, and the overpowering regulatory authority of The State (government). Examples from the previous pages included: The State (representing the authority of government), marriage and family, religion, labor and a free press.

We have looked at examples of specific violations of each of the spheres and the unintended consequences that resulted. The main point to keep in mind is that government, by its very nature, will tend to grow, violating the sanctity of societal spheres that are meant to limit its power to regulate every aspect of human life. Failing to recognize that God, not man, is the creator of all that was, is, and will ever be is to be trapped in the subtlest of lies.

"In him all things were created: things in heaven and on earth, visible and invisible, whether thrones or

powers or rulers or authorities; all things have been created through him and for him." (Colossians 1:16)

So, having examined the consequences of six lies that have divided America along the fault line of two incompatible worldviews, what would God have us do?

To gain eternal life, we must be free of sin. Sin cannot enter into heaven. *"Nothing impure will ever enter it, nor will anyone who does what is shameful or deceitful, but only those whose names are written in the Lamb's book of life."* (Revelation 21:27) We can't remove our guilt on our own, but our sins can be forgiven. Jesus, the only innocent One, gave his life for that purpose.

Our transgressions are forgiven if we do three things. First, we must confess our sins. With honest regret and in humility we acknowledge how far short we have fallen. Second, we publicly declare that Jesus is our Lord and Savior. Third, we ask that the Holy Spirit come to dwell in us and replace our imperfect human conscience.

This is the beginning of a Christian's walk of faith. Beyond these three steps, becoming a Christian requires fellowship with other believers, prayer, the study of scripture, worship, and the use of one's spiritual gifts dedicated to serving others for God's glory. It ain't easy! Christians soon learn that each day they must deny themselves, submitting, sacrificing their will in favor of God's will for their lives. Discipleship requires commitment beyond tithes and occupying a seat on Sunday morning.

It's a mistake to believe that accepting God's mercy and grace guarantees protection from injustice, pain, loss, loneliness, sickness, or poverty. Any hardship that befalls all of humanity can certainly fall upon the lives of the faithful. *"You have heard that it was said, love your neighbor and hate your enemy. But I tell you, love your enemies and pray for those who persecute you, that you may be children of your Father in heaven. He causes his sun to rise on the evil and the good and sends rain on the righteous and the unrighteous."* (Matthew 5:40-45)

Created by God, in His image, we are failing to trust in His authority; choosing to believe a lie that severed our relationship with Him. We serve our punishment living in a fallen world ruled by Satan, the father of all lies. But, God loves us, has given us commandments, moral and ethical standards by which we're to lead our lives, and the freedom to choose our own path. As a species, we are wont to do what we want to do. It's habitual to our very nature to do that which we desire, and that's often in conflict with what God has ordained.

As any father loving his children, God wants what's best for each of us, offering correction when we go wrong, but respecting our individual sovereignty, allowing us to make our own choices and stand accountable for them.

In America today, this part of the relationship is one that gets too little attention. Many want God's love and pray to Him to shower them with all manner of blessings, but they don't want to consider being held accountable for choices that clearly reject His will and His purpose for their lives. No. What we see too often is whining and crying and gnashing of teeth when life goes haywire and the blame is with God. Our unbelief is enough to convict us.

Our Father in heaven has given all authority over heaven and earth to the Son, Jesus, and he has no need, nor desire to condemn us to hell. His judgment is based solely on our faithfulness as defined by our choices throughout our lives. In the *Preface*, the question was posed: When faced with a sorely divided people, corruption and failure in high places, will a democratic republic, constituted on principles of equality for all, under the law, a government of the people and by the people, confront the lie that can destroy? We understand, then, not only do individuals stand accountable before our Creator, but nations must also answer for their collective obedience or disobedience.

Twenty-first century America is headed in the wrong direction. If we as individual citizens continue to actively promote, or condone (by our silence), the godless moral and ethical decay, the descent of our nation's soul, we surely will be inviting God's judgment.

God has blessed America. What has been achieved by way of technology, health care, and opportunity is beyond remarkable. This unprecedented achievement has revealed that our leaders are vulnerable. Too many in Washington, and those who lead on Wall Street, and others across our country occupying positions of influence have unwittingly been taken captive by the lie.

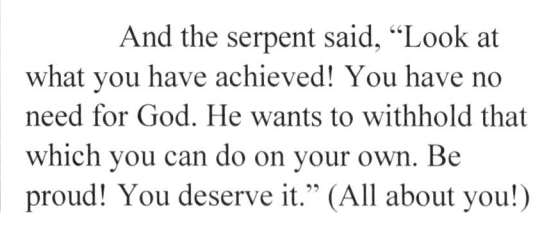

And the serpent said, "Look at what you have achieved! You have no need for God. He wants to withhold that which you can do on your own. Be proud! You deserve it." (All about you!)

History and the *Holy Bible* teach that godless nations are destroyed. In Genesis 17:6-10, God promised the Land of Israel to Abraham and his descendants. *"I will make you very fruitful; I will make nations of you, and kings will come from you. I will establish my covenant as an everlasting covenant between me and you and your descendants ... for the generations to come ... The whole land of Canaan ... I will give as an everlasting possession to you and your descendants after you; and I will be their God."*

Years later, in Numbers 13:1-2, The Israelites, led by Moses, were ready to enter Canaan, the Promised Land. God tells Moses to send spies into the land of Canaan and check it out. *"The LORD spoke to Moses saying, 'Send out for yourself men so that they may spy out the land of Canaan, which I am going to give to the sons of Israel.'"*

Moses did as God said and sent one leader from each of the twelve tribes. After forty days they returned; they reported that the land did flow with milk and honey, but there were fearsome men living there including the Amalekites living in the desert; the Hittites, Jebusites and Amorites living in the hill country and the Canaanites near the sea and along the Jordan river, all of them powerful and well defended. (See Numbers 13:25-33)

God was prepared to fulfill His promise to Abraham, but then issued a stern reminder. *"It shall come about if you ever forget the LORD your God and go after other gods and serve them and worship them, I testify against you today that you will surely perish. Like the nations that the LORD makes to perish before you, so you shall perish; because you would not listen to the voice of the LORD your God."* (Deuteronomy 8:19-20)

As He promised, all the nations of that land were defeated, allowing the Israelites to take possession of the land, but they did not obey His command to *"destroy them totally."* The remnants that remained corrupted the people and they turned their backs to God committing murder, and adultery, and offering up human sacrifices to pagan gods.

A prophet, Jeremiah, gave warning to the people of Israel concerning their disobedience.

"This is what the Lord Almighty, the God of Israel, says: Go ahead, add your burnt offerings to your other sacrifices and eat the meat yourselves! For when I brought your ancestors out of Egypt and spoke to them, I did not just give them commands about burnt offerings and sacrifices, but I gave them this command: Obey me, and I will be your God and you will be my people."

"Walk in obedience to all I command you, that it may go well with you. But they did not listen or pay attention; instead, they followed the stubborn inclinations of their evil hearts."

"When you tell them all this, they will not listen to you; when you call to them, they will not answer. Therefore, say to them, 'This is the nation that has not obeyed the LORD its God or responded to correction. Truth has perished; it has vanished from their lips." (Jeremiah 7:20-27)

In 425 BC, the Babylonians, led by Nebuchadnezzar marched on Jerusalem with the intent of its total destruction. All the warnings had failed to change the hearts of the people. Their king, Zedekiah, was brutally taken captive. Without regard for age or gender, people were slaughtered by the sword. Thousands died. The walls of Jerusalem were torn down, the Temple was set ablaze, the riches of the empire established by King David and his son, King Solomon, were carried off to Babylon. God had loosed His wrath on the disobedience of Judah.

This is not to be taken as a prophesy for America; we observe it only to affirm that God does intervene in the affairs of nations and their leaders. Since the Jewish State of Israel was established in 1948, America has remained a loyal ally with Israel, providing billions in financial and military assistance. Recently, President Donald Trump, moved the United States Embassy from Tel Aviv to Jerusalem in a show of support for Israel's sovereignty.

It was a controversial move drawing protests from Palestinian supporters at home and abroad. Many are offended by the Jews being called the "Chosen People." It's God's call. Who is going to tell Him otherwise?

"Now the Lord said to Abram, "Go out from your country, your relatives, and your father's household to the land that I will show you. Then I will make you into a great nation, and I will bless you, and I will make your name great, in order that you might be a prime example of divine blessing. I will bless those who bless you, but the one who treats you lightly I must curse." (Genesis 12:1-3)

You may be asking, what's the point of all this? America should support the nation of Israel. America's roots are in the Christian faith, the faith of our Forefathers. Jesus, by birth, is a Jew. He is the Christ (Messiah). Christians form the body of Christ on earth. We should resist any attempt to say otherwise. America should never break its bond with Israel. God will curse those who go against His people.

How we treat Israel is one thing. How God judges our rejection of His moral authority is quite another. Christians, congregations and clergy, have largely remained silent while our nation's leaders, the appointed and the elected, continue to lead in opposition to God's word. The evidence is clear.

1962 (*Engle v. Vitale*) Justice Hugo Black handed down the 6-1 vote of the Supreme Court ruling that any kind of prayer, composed by public school districts, even non-denominational prayer, is government sponsorship of religion, therefore, unconstitutional. (Isn't there a difference between sponsoring an activity and allowing it?)

1963. (*Abington School District v. Schempp*) Justice Clark wrote the opinion for the 8-1 majority that public schools are prohibited from sponsoring bible readings and recitations of the *Lord's Prayer* as they violate the *First Amendment's* establishment clause. (As an educator, rather than disallow fundamental religious activity, I see natural opportunities within this case to teach, engage students and adults in learning, about religions other than their own. Why are our leaders so frightened of allowing us to share our beliefs about matters of the human spirit? Sharing doesn't mean indoctrinating. To learn about communism doesn't mean I'll become a communist.) Religious instruction should be the heart of public education!

1973 (*Roe v. Wade*) Chief Justice, Warren Burger, handed down the 7-2 ruling of the Supreme Court that has resulted in estimates by the *U.S. Abortion Clock.org.* that 60 million lives have been snuffed out through the process of legalized abortion. I will not judge. In all humility I can only say that those saying they respect human life surely cannot justify this process. (There is a difference between having an opinion and passing judgment.)

2003 (*Lawrence v. Texas*) the U.S. Supreme Court in a 6–3 decision struck down the Texas same-sex sodomy law.

2013 (*United States v. Windsor*) The 1996 *Defense of Marriage Act* was declared unconstitutional by a 5-4 vote of the Supreme Court. to be in violation of the rights of those who declare themselves as gays and lesbians.

2015 (Obergefell et al. v. Hodges) the Supreme Court ruled that state level bans on same-sex marriage were unconstitutional, overturning all previous decisions to the contrary. The Court ruled 5-4 that the process clause and the equal protection clause of the *Fourteenth Amendment* required all fifty states to allow same-sex couples to marry and grant them the same legal rights and responsibilities as between a man and woman.

Five cases, all reflecting humanism a social-progressive point of view favoring popular "modern" opinion, ignoring established social norms that have existed for centuries and the words of the *Constitution of the United States* and the instructions of the *Holy Bible*. These cases are rife with examples of substituting one's subjective personal bias for objective unbiased attention to the rule of law. Christians are caught in the middle. Whose law shall we follow?

"And if at another time I announce that a nation or kingdom is to be built up and planted, and if it does evil in my sight and does not obey me, then I will reconsider the good I had intended to do for it." (Jeremiah 18: 9-10)

"The leaders of this people cause them to err, and those who are led by them are destroyed" (Isaiah 9:16)

We've been critical of the Supreme Court, (justly I think) but in fairness, there's plenty of blame to go around. We can't be guilty of pointing at the Court without acknowledging that in pointing the finger of blame, there are three fingers pointing back at us. The Court has not always upheld the strict interpretation of separation of church and state. In *Zorach v. Clauson* (1952), Justice William Douglas wrote that releasing students from school to receive religious instruction did not violate either the free exercise of religion clause or the establishment of religion clause. That was more than a half-century ago, but it's a beacon of hope that common sense can prevail.

If America continues to drift toward a humanist-socialist worldview, a society governed according to man's sense of what is ethical and moral, as opposed to the Word of God, the Christian worldview along with those of other religious faiths will be at the mercy of a government that believes religion is the enemy.

The increasing challenge for believers will be to mobilize in ways that reflect the spiritual power of the Church. On this soil, believers are the body of Christ's Church. We can't afford to sit on our hands waiting for unbelievers to acknowledge us. Those who have been born again should reflect on what motivated them to give their lives to Christ. Was it only to avoid eternal damnation for rejecting the life of God's only son?

Pastor Bruce Bendinger, *New Beginnings Community Church*, Franklin, IN believes we should ask ourselves that question to clarify our purpose. He gave us the following remarks to ponder:

"If being saved is only about avoiding eternal separation from God, that would be like preparing for a life-long career, but upon completion of the requirements, you retire! Once we've confessed our sins, and accepted Jesus as Lord of our lives, it's not time to retire. It's time to get to work! We're called to use our God-given spiritual gifts to make life on this earth better for our families, friends, neighbors, and those who persecute us—remember, love your enemies, pray for them, forgive them while holding them accountable for any harm they do."

As I pondered what Pastor Bruce had said, it became clear to me that so many of us are satisfied to be comfortable in our faith. We're saved. We attend church most Sundays, put our coppers in the collection plate as it passes down the pew, "volunteer" when called upon, and in our prayers, we give thanks and ask for God to bless us. We're good Christians.

But, you know what? The more I pondered the more I realized that Jesus isn't messin' around. While on earth, he was on a serious mission. He cited twenty or more reasons why he came. I didn't find any that said he came to make us comfortable or take early retirement. No. As Pastor Bruce said, "After we're saved, it's time to go to work." So, now is the time.

Now is the Time! It's time for Christians to take a stand, united in the Word of God, where race, gender, age, politics count for nothing because we stand by His grace alone, delivered from darkness by the love, obedience, forgiveness, humility, and blood of Jesus, the Christ.

Now is the time! It's time for Christians to recommit our hearts, minds, and bodies to fulfilling our Creator's purpose for our lives individually and collectively. That purpose being to love Him, and to love our neighbors as we love ourselves, to forgive others that we might be forgiven, and to go, using our spiritual gifts, making disciples in the name of the One given all power and authority in this world.

Now is the time! It's time for Christians to grasp the threat. The culture of politics in America is sick and the Supreme Court has declared religion is the enemy of government. If the Supreme Court continues to hold to the invalid clause "impregnable wall of separation" between Church and State, people of faith will be run over, trampled by laws favoring pagan unbelievers. Where God is denied, paganism fills the void. If believers stand silent on fundamental social issues, (marriage & family, freedom of religion, speech, and assembly) the tyranny of the humanist-socialist agenda will silence the voice of the Church. Our voice has already been censored!

Now is the time! It's time for Christians and other faith groups to be accountable, standing strong, united against further attacks on religious freedom and the freedom of speech. When called for, a message to government, businesses, and/or associations, firmly proclaiming that God's word "compels us (me) to address this issue" and using scripture to validate the claim. This would put whoever or whatever on notice that threats to free speech or religious liberty, intentionally or unintentionally, would be confronted by a unified Church. The Church commands that the Law above the law is to be respected. If necessary, the faithful can exercise the power of the purse—economic sanctions.

Now is the time! It's time for Christians to rethink what it means to be a true disciple of the One who paid the price to redeem our lost souls. We're given a second chance to use our spiritual gifts in the service of those in need, and to be a lamp unto the feet of unbelievers before their blindness leads them into destruction. The ranks of the walking wounded pass by us every day.

Now is the time! It's time for Christians to recognize the power in numbers. Who is supposed to articulate the Christian worldview, if not Christians? Leadership is needed to organize the body of Christ in developing a national strategy, that includes unambiguous goals, achievable objectives leading to the attainment of our purpose—serving others. The best way to articulate one's position is to dialogue with someone who disagrees.

Now is the time! It's time for Christians to prepare themselves for battle; it's coming. Keep your eyes on *Antifa*. This is an anti-America movement, well-funded, with the intent "by any means necessary," of destroying the United States from within. Their slogan: "No border, no wall, no USA at all!" Our way of life is at stake. Know the *Constitution*. Prepare to act; encourage others to do the same. We can speak, write, run for office, campaign for those who support a Christian worldview—remain humble, forgive, invite, pray, and work together for God's glory.

Now is the time! It's time for more Christians to come off the sidelines and get in the game! Men and women of faith, whose spiritual gifts would enable them to <u>serve</u> in government should be encouraged to do so. Jesus said he did not come to be served, but to serve. <u>(Mark 10: 45)</u> The concept of servant leadership is biblical.

The power of love—moral and ethical persuasion by candidates representing a religious worldview could overcome the shrill shouts and empty slogans of those who claim to love peace, but march to the beat of violence and intolerance against those who seek to obey the laws of God.

Now is the time! It's time for Christians to double-down on our works. Our works must speak for themselves. There has to be ample evidence to convince skeptics that Christians really are attending to the needs of the poor, the elderly, the homeless, the addicted, and the emotionally scarred. Let our energy, spirit, and benevolence in our communities be enough to remove the scales from the eyes of unbelievers who see only our hypocrisy. Let our works shame the government for treating us as the enemy. If religion has no works, its protests are empty.

Now is the Time! It's time for Christians to write to their legislators and governors in support of calling a "Convention of States" as defined in *Article V* of the *Constitution*. Amendments to the *Constitution* may be proposed when "deemed necessary ... upon the application of the legislatures of two-thirds of the states." Proposed amendments upon being "ratified by three-fourths of the states, shall be valid, to all intents and purposes,"... "as part of this Constitution."

Retired Oklahoma Senator Tom Coburn (R), has stated, "One of the reasons I left was because I no longer believe that Washington is capable of reining itself in ... the only avenue to change is the one given to us by our Founders in the *Constitution—Article V,* Convention of States, where the people, not the politicians, are in charge."

Anyone paying the slightest attention to what is happening in America must agree with Sen. Coburn. The career politicians in Congress will never voluntarily call for any change that would threaten their power or golden parachute retirement plan. Religious liberty and powers once delegated to the states, have been trampled, usurped by Congress and the Supreme Court. Restoring the original intent of government by the people will be a difficult fight. Our Forefathers understood, even predicted it.

George Mason, VA, understanding that no amendments could be proposed from a tyrannical federal government, is credited with recommending that the states have a means by which they can achieve amendments to the *Constitution, "when deemed necessary,"* not limited by any of the three branches, that is the essence of *Article V*.

This is a bipartisan issue. It's time for us—We the People, to reclaim our authority to accomplish what the government is unwilling to do. Getting thirty-four governors and state legislatures to convene for this purpose is a daunting task. For information: info@cosaction.co, Also available at www.Facebook.com/ConventionOfStates.

Now is the Time! It's time for Christians to attend to the state of affairs in our public schools. Our Forefathers understood the importance of having a well-educated, civil society based on the values taught from the *Holy Bible* and the proposition of self-control. As we discussed earlier, it was 1963 when the Supreme Court outlawed Bible readings in public schools, since that time the emphasis shifted from instruction based on a religious worldview to a humanist-socialist worldview. "God is dead," became the mantra of unbelievers. It has taken hold in our schools. Students are instructed only in those liberal values that embrace humanist-socialism and honor racial and sexual diversity at the expense of national unity. This has become a flash point that is tearing America apart.

In November 1999, a group of twenty organizations including boards of education, teachers, attorneys and religious groups representing the Judeo-Christian faith, acting together, issued a consensus statement: *The Bible & Public Schools, A First Amendment Guide*. It reveals that the Court made the following observation: "It certainly may be said that the Bible is worthy for study for its literary and historic qualities. Nothing we have said here *(Abington v. Schempp, 1963)* indicates that such study of the Bible or of religion, when presented objectively as part of a secular education, may not be effectively consistent with the *First Amendment.*" (For information: www.*The Bible's Influence: The Bible & Public Schools – Washington Times*)

I have indeed, been hard on the Court, but in the above statement it provided a legal way for schools to use religion and the Bible as a means to educate young minds by introducing them to major historical and literary narratives, symbols and characters from the Bible and discover how these have influenced contemporary music, books, poetry drama, civil rights, and our legal system.

If local schools are not taking advantage of this contingency, Christians can influence local boards of education to investigate the potential of this opportunity. Religion need not be the enemy of government or education. It should be the foundation of both.

"And from childhood you have known the sacred writings which are able to give you the wisdom that leads to salvation through faith which is in Christ Jesus. All Scripture is inspired by God and profitable for teaching, for reproof, for correction, for training in righteousness." (2 Timothy 3:15-16)

Now is the time! It's time for Christians to be bold. People of faith at all levels, professionals in every field, factory workers, farmers, sales people, be vigilant, step forward to protect the Judeo/Christian worldview. In the extreme, we may be called to resist man's laws that violate our faith values.

Dr. Martin Luther King wrote in his *Letter from the Birmingham Jail*, "One has a moral responsibility to disobey unjust laws." Protest beyond the law is not a departure from democracy; it is absolutely essential to it. He explained, "Just law is man-made in agreement with the law of God, the moral law. An unjust law is one out of harmony with the moral law." Dr. King was arrested frequently, standing accountable for his actions. A man of

God, he walked the talk. His dignity and courage shamed the values and actions of his enemies. Jesus is not a wimp. He stood in defiance of the authorities and was arrested because his message threatened those who made the laws. If called, should we do less? It's not child's play.

One last point, if required to make our voices heard, here's the key. Unlike *Antifa*, and other organized protesters hiding their shame behind masks, bricks, fires, broken glass, firearms, wanton destruction of property, and physical violence are never to be associated with protests by those claiming to be disciples of Christ. Jesus will not approve of bullying, threatening, cursing, or shouting insults at those we need to reach.

Throughout this book we've emphasized the battle of worldviews—the cosmic battle for America's soul. Actually, it's a world-wide battle, an eternal fight for the souls of God's rebellious children. Good v. evil, the Light v. darkness, the Truth v. lies, the battle is not over.

Christians, true disciples, and religious leaders with courage, conviction, and integrity must be willing to put Truth before popularity, willing to stand up for their faith, defend it, live it—and in the extreme, die for it. The time may be sooner than we think. Will we be ready?

"By this all will know that you are My disciples, if you have love for one another." (John 13-35

THE LIE AND

THE LIGHT

America/Divided

Do you know your spiritual gifts?

CRAFTSMANSHIP
APOSTLESHIP
ENCOURAGING
DISCERNMENT
ADMINISTRATION
GIVING
FAITH
MERCY
HEALING
PROPHESY
MIRACLES WISDOM
LEADERSHIP
TEACHING
EVANGELIM SHEPHERDING
KNOWLEDGE

God, in His great wisdom, has given each of us specific talents, gifts we can use to fulfill His purpose. In obedience we glorify the Glorifier.

About the Author:

Books by Jim

The Gift: *Poetry and Prose* (2015)

Testimony of the King: *20 Reasons Jesus Came to Earth* (2016)

Dark Souls: *Subscribing to Evil* (2017) Adventure & History

At Amazonbooks.com and other book stores.

Jim Ellsberry, Prince's Lakes, IN, was born in Terre Haute in 1936, Graduate of Garfield High School (1954), Indiana State University, B.S. (1958), M.S. (1960), Michigan State University Ed. S. (1964) Honorable discharge from the United States Army (1963)

    He and Doris were married in 1961, raised one son and three daughters, have three grandchildren, and recently became great grandparents. His career as teacher, counselor, coach and administrator included experiences ranging in scope from K-12 in the public schools, to higher education, including years at Butler University and Indiana Wesleyan University, Elder, New Beginnings Community Church, Franklin, IN

    Fishing, yard work, golf, writing, and following the Colts, Pacers, Butler Bulldogs, Cardinals, and Cubs on TV—life is good!

Praise God from whom all blessings flow!

Made in the USA
Columbia, SC
17 January 2019